D0049958

Praise for *The Western Guide to Feng Shui*

The Western Guide to Feng Shui *is a fascinating collection of many stories about the positive changes that have occurred in people's lives after making Feng Shui adjustments.* The Western Guide to Feng Shui *is highly recommended for all metaphysical reference book collections.*
— **The Midwest Book Review**
Wisconsin Book Watch

A Feng Shui teacher and consultant, Terah Kathryn Collins has written a clear guide to help Westerners understand and work with the energies that are mapped by this system.
— **Napra ReView**

There are many books on the market now that endeavor to explain the ancient Chinese art of placement, Feng Shui. This detailed guide stands out from the rest because it provides practical applications of Feng Shui principles to the Western world.
— **Branches**

Terah Kathryn Collins has created a step-by-step approach for Feng Shui novices. She embraces holistic values and encourages readers to contemplate the meaning and value of chi. Each chapter ends with one or two meditative exercises designed to enhance a reader's own perception of his of her immediate surroundings.
— **Country Living Magazine**

Please visit the Hay House Website at
http://www.hayhouse.com

▼▼▼

THE WESTERN GUIDE
TO FENG SHUI

Creating Balance, Harmony, and Prosperity
in Your Environment

Terah Kathryn Collins

Hay House, Inc.
Carlsbad, CA

Copyright © 1996 by Terah Kathryn Collins
Published and distributed in the United States by:
Hay House, Inc., P.O. Box 5100, Carlsbad, CA 92018-5100
(800) 654-5126

Edited by:	Jill Kramer	
Designed by:	Carylee Stone, Coastline Graphics	Del Mar, CA
Calligraphy by:	Rosemary KimBal, Dancing Brush	Cardiff, CA
Drawings by:	Cheryl Rice, Cheryl Rice Interiors	La Jolla, CA

All rights reserved. No part of this book may be reproduced by any mechanical, photographic, or electronic process, or in the form of a phonographic recording, nor may it be stored in a retrieval system, transmitted, or otherwise be copied for public or private use—other than for "fair use" as brief quotations embodied in articles and reviews without prior written permission of the publisher.

Library of Congress Cataloging-in-Publication Data

Collins, Terah Kathryn.
    The western guide to feng shui : creating balance, harmony, and
    prosperity in your environment / Terah Kathryn Collins.
        p.   cm.
    Includes bibliographical references.
    ISBN 1-56170-324-9 (trade paper)
        1. Feng-shui.   2. Interior decoration   3. Architecture, Domestic.
    I. Title.
    BF1779.F4K335   1996
    133.3'33—dc20   95-47274
                                                                        CIP

ISBN 1-56170-324-9

00 99 98 97   17 16 15 14

First Printing, March 1996
Fourteenth Printing, July 1997

Printed in the United States of America

To our homes and workplaces.
May they be our Personal Paradises.

TABLE OF
CONTENTS

- Getting Carried Away—Bathrooms
- Mapping the Bagua of Your Furniture

My Own
Journey Home

I began my Feng Shui journey when a friend insisted that I join her at a lecture on a strange subject called Feng Shui. I had heard just enough about it to assume it was a superstitious collection of Chinese folklore. Now I was invited to sit through an evening lecture on it. Reluctantly, I went.

Dr. Richard Tan was the speaker, a highly respected acupuncturist and Feng Shui expert in San Diego, California. I was in my seat less than three minutes when I was filled with the realization that Feng Shui described what I had been intuitively practicing for years. It was one of those rare and wonderful moments when I felt that my whole life had been arranged in perfect sequence to bring me to this man and this information. As I listened to Dr. Tan, my excitement about, and awe of, the synchronicities in life steadily grew. Here was an ancient Eastern science that approached and treated buildings in the same holistic manner that I had approached and treated people for over a decade. Wide awake and hanging on Dr. Tan's every word, I took my first lesson in the theory and practice of Feng Shui—the language of my future.

I immersed myself in the study of Feng Shui with Dr. Tan; with Louis Audet, a Feng Shui expert with a rich understanding of Earth Wisdom practices; and with Master Lin Yun, a Feng Shui authority and founder of the Yun Lin Temple in Berkeley, California. As I studied with different teachers and read everything on Feng Shui that I could get my hands on, I observed that tightly woven into the timeless fabric of Feng Shui, were the holistic principles I had always worked with and lived by. And for the first time in my life, I felt passionately in love with what I was doing, and aligned with my life's purpose.

The search for my life's purpose began when I was a teenager. I learned and practiced transcendental meditation and yoga, took instruction from the I Ching, and studied Eastern philosophy. After high school, I decided to travel and perhaps live in other areas of the world. I lived in South America, then Puerto Rico, the American Southwest, and finally, Spain. Throughout my journeys, I experienced countless synchronicities, including an endless stream of people involved in holistic health. It became the ongoing theme of my travels. Chiropractors, acupuncturists, shamans, and healers of all kinds crossed my path, sharing their ways of bringing people back into healthful balance.

Inspired by my adventures, four years later, I returned to my home in Virginia and became a registered polarity practitioner and neurolinguistic programmer, honing the skills of holistic health provider and educator. This led to a busy practice in holistic health care, as well as co-founding (and teaching at) the Polarity Therapy Center of Northern Virginia.

Time passed, and one day during a meditation, I was struck by the fact that it had been 14 years since I'd returned to Virginia from my travels—and that it was, again, time to move on. I sensed a significant change coming in my profession as well. It was time to take the steps necessary to go where I'd always wanted to be—California. I began preparing that day.

For the next two years, I carefully brought all areas of my life to completion. I trained an apprentice to take over my practice, turned my teaching responsibilities over to my partner, and spent as much time as possible with my friends and family. Finally, I closed the door on the moving van and headed for California.

After I settled in San Diego, I faced the next challenge—what now? I didn't feel moved to start another practice, or teach as I had before. I felt something new was coming, and I couldn't re-immerse myself in the past. I was captivated by the notion that holistic health principles apply as powerfully to environments as they do to people. With this in mind, I felt that my new purpose would involve healing and my love for the environment. I filled notebooks with correlations, musings, and notes on my observations of "the environmental body." I felt pregnant with myself and prayed to be "delivered" so that I could move forward with my life. What is my new profession? When will it be born?

The delivery came unexpectedly (as is often the case), at Dr. Tan's lecture. Suddenly, in the middle of a classroom, I was giving birth to my own future—Feng Shui.

— Terah Kathryn Collins
San Diego, CA 1996

▼▼▼

ACKNOWLEDGMENTS

Just as it takes a community to raise a child, it takes a community to write a book. This book has been written by the loving and supportive community of people I call my friends and family.

My special thanks and eternal gratitude to Alice and Whit Beatson, Arnold Patent, Pam King, Arlene Swope, Dr. Richard Tan, Louis Audet, Master Lin Yun, Sarah Rossbach, Eddie Baumruk, and Evelyn Thomas, Ron Tillinghast, Jill Kramer, Lisa Roth, Marilyn Felter, Michael Karsh, Cheryl Rice, Jackie and Richard Earnest, Mary Lou LoPreste, Shivam Kohls, Dale and Blanca Schusterman, Rosemary KimBal, and Carylee Stone.

And to Louise Hay, who fueled me with her humor and guided me along the writer's path, encouraging me a hundred times or more to "just keep writing!"

And to my husband and the father of this book, Brian Collins, who embraces me every day with his love, support, and pure enthusiasm. His lightness of being and natural understanding of Feng Shui are largely responsible for the ease and joy with which this book was born.

INTRODUCTION

This book is a practical guide for people in Western cultures on how to apply and benefit from the ancient wisdom found in Feng Shui (pronounced *FUNG SHWAY*), the Chinese Art of Placement. This guide is not a complete treatise on the subject of Feng Shui. Rather, it concentrates on giving clear, concise explanations of Feng Shui principles and treatments that address the specific needs of our Western lifestyle. When I look through my "Feng Shui Eyes"—eyes that perceive the Ch'i (pronounced *CHEE*) or energy in and around our physical world— I see that the need is great.

Early in my career as a Feng Shui consultant, I was asked by a real estate broker to take a look at six properties that had been on the market for over a year and had not sold. In all six, there were glaring Feng Shui problems. In one, there was something stored behind every door, making it impossible to freely move in and out of any of the rooms. In another, a staircase ran directly toward the front door, while furniture and clutter blocked smooth passage through the house.

I unblocked thresholds, moved furniture, balanced architectural problems, softened corners, and made many recommendations of things to do, undo, add, and subtract, that would lift and enhance the Ch'i. I hoped that the improvements I was suggesting would make the homes more attractive to potential buyers. What happened was a big surprise to me *and* the real estate broker. Within the next 30 days, 4 of the 6 owners took their homes off the market because they fell in love with them all over again and decided they didn't want to move after all. Meanwhile, the other two homes sold within the same time period. I can still remember the shocked look on the broker's face as we talked over the results. Since she couldn't rely on Feng Shui to produce lucrative results for her real estate business (what if all six had been taken off the market?), she wasn't interested in "Feng Shui-ing" her listed houses in the future. But she'd certainly give Feng Shui consultations as housewarming gifts!

Since this remarkable incident occurred with the real estate broker, I have worked on hundreds of homes and offices. Although the name "Feng Shui" often seems mysterious and foreign to people in Western cultures, it's actually a very sensible collection of ideas and action steps that make perfect sense to anyone who approaches the world in a holistic manner. Feng Shui is based on the premise that people experience happier, healthier, more prosperous lives when their home and work environments are harmonious. As with human bodies, the "healthier" the bodies of our buildings are, the more they support us in living a rich, creative, joyful existence. People often exclaim that the changes I'm suggesting are so obvious—*why hadn't they thought of them before?!*

For many of you, understanding the principles of Feng Shui is just "one click of the mental dial" away. With this guide and some serious practice, you can produce harmony, comfort, and balance in almost any environment—including a crowded office, tract home, or condominium. You can diagnose and heal your home or workplace, often in the face of severe architectural imbalances, land injuries, and discordant building choices that were made in the past. The answers are often simple and sensible. You just need to open your Feng Shui eyes and take a look around.

This book gives instruction on a new way of seeing. It introduces you to the intriguing concepts of Ch'i, yin and yang, and the five elements that are so helpful when diagnosing and balancing your environment. You will learn how to "read" and correct problematic locations and structural features. This book also offers many practical suggestions and examples on how to place and arrange the material objects in your life—from your front door to your desk—to enhance your happiness and success. It discusses the ways you can charge up your environment with items that are easy to find and wonderful to live with. This book also explains the Bagua (pronounced *BAHG-WAH*) Map, a remarkable tool you can use to produce positive changes in your personal and professional life. Throughout the book, you will find many stories about people's experiences that further illustrate Feng Shui principles in action.

Enjoy exploring your own surroundings through Feng Shui eyes. It is a journey into yourself, the places where you spend most of your time, and the essential quality of your life!

WHEN TO APPLY FENG SHUI

Apply the Principles of Feng Shui When:

- You are designing and building a new home or office building.
- You are choosing an existing home or business location for lease or purchase.
- You are remodeling or building an addition onto an existing home or workplace.
- You are planning to sell a building or a piece of land.
- You would like to increase your prosperity, enhance your relationships, boost your health, or upgrade your life in any way.
- You notice your life has changed in some important way since you moved into your current home or office.
- You would like to bless the building you live or work in.

Paradise is where I am.

–Voltaire

1

FENG SHUI, THE CHINESE ART OF PLACEMENT

Feng Shui, a Chinese term meaning "Wind and Water," predates Confucianism and Taoism, and has been practiced for over three thousand years in China. Early practitioners of Feng Shui located building sites for homes and villages. An auspicious site was one where the vital energy called *Ch'i* flowed in a manner that was harmonious and supportive of human life.

Feng Shui practitioners relied on their highly tuned senses, their intuition, and the knowledge passed down from their teachers to assess the land. They were interpreters of sorts, translating the dialect of a mountain, valley, or meadow into the language that local villagers could understand and benefit from. In this way they were responsible for strategically placing habitats above flood plains, below strong winds, and in the safe embrace of land that was blessed with harmonious Ch'i.

Often called the "belly of the dragon," a classically harmonious configuration of land was much like the shape of an armchair. The pre-

ferred plot for building sat on even ground, and was embraced and pro-
tected in back and around both sides by mountains, hills, or a forest,
similar to the back and armrests of a chair. The land then descended to
a lower level in front of the plot, where a river, stream, pond, or lake
completed the ideal location.

Feng Shui practitioners paid close attention to the intuitive impressions that they received as they "joined" with the land and felt its Ch'i
qualities. They listened to every sound, tasted the soil, scouted the surrounding area, observed the contours of the land, looked for the telltale
patterns made by wind and water, and watched for omens. Every physical feature and condition communicated the quality of the surrounding
Ch'i. Animal bones, dead trees, and sharp protruding or waterworn
rocks were often considered bad omens, while vibrant foliage, meandering streams, and living game animals symbolized good fortune,
health, and happiness for the people who would live there.

Once a suitable plot of land was located, the Feng Shui practitioner guided the building process so that the benevolent qualities of the
Ch'i were not damaged in any way. They chose the building materials
and monitored every step of construction to assure that the Ch'i continued to flow in a friendly, nourishing manner. The building was like a
jewel being placed in its perfect setting. One wrong move could harm
or destroy the delicate Ch'i balance between the manmade structure and
its natural surroundings.

Western Feng Shui

To practice Feng Shui today, we need to blend traditional Feng Shui
wisdom with our own keen intuitive, investigative, diagnostic, and
communicative skills. Our Western habitats present us with a very different scenario than that of the original Feng Shui practitioners. Many
structures are located on land that the ancient practitioners would never
have chosen, and often the structure's shape and detailing break every
classic Feng Shui rule.

Instead of finding the perfect plot of land to develop gently, we usually start with a structure that already exists. If the builders were not

careful, they disturbed the natural Ch'i that circulated around the property. We find that in most cases we are unable to control the location, the direction, or the configuration of other buildings and streets in the area. This presents the Western Feng Shui practitioner with a new set of challenges. We are rarely dealt a perfect hand. However, when we apply Feng Shui principles, we find that we have quite a deck of powerful, results-producing ways to enhance the Ch'i and establish harmony in our environments. Whether the direction is north, south, east, or west, whether the location is inner city or rural mountaintop, whether the intent is business success or residential harmony, the healthy flow of Ch'i is always crucial. Just like human beings, no two buildings are alike in form or function. The challenge and the joy in Feng Shui is to balance the meridians or pathways of Ch'i in our individual homes and offices to achieve the desired result—health, prosperity, and happiness.

You can be your own Feng Shui practitioner. The art and science of Feng Shui gives you a big bag of tools to help you produce positive results in your environments. Practice working with them, and instead of wondering what you can do to improve your surroundings, you will see with your Feng Shui eyes exactly what to do. You will know precisely where to "tap."

Feng Shui, Here and Now

Experience has taught me to apply Feng Shui principles wherever I am. This means that a rental apartment, leased office, hotel room, or any "temporary" quarters still needs to be balanced. I find it tremendously helpful to enhance the Ch'i in even the most temporary accommodations, such as in the places where I hold workshops or spend a few nights when traveling (see Traveling Feng Shui, page 183).

Many people look forward to applying Feng Shui to their new homes—as soon as they *buy* them. But, they feel it's a waste of time and money to fix up rentals they'll be in for just a year or two. This is like saying, "I'm going to wait a year or two to take good care of myself." Lodging or office space that has Ch'i-depleting qualities can drain the resources of those who live or work there, whether temporary or not. On the other hand, a Ch'i-enriched environment attracts all kinds of benefits and positive opportunities. If your goal is to buy a house, or simply to live a good life, it is wise to do everything in your power to create a personal paradise, right here, right now. The Ch'i that moves through the spaces where you live and work NOW is of vital importance to your health, prosperity, and happiness. So, begin where you are. Balancing and enhancing the environment where you find yourself today is one of the best ways to energize and manifest your goals, hopes, and dreams for the future.

Being born with good looks is
   not as important as being born
   with a good destiny;

Being born with a good destiny
   is not as important as having a
   kind heart;

Having a kind heart is not as
   important as having a
   positive state of Ch'i.

–Chinese saying

CHARTING
THE SEA OF CH'I

There are three basic principles that form the foundation on which Feng Shui is built. These principles define Ch'i, the vital energy that animates, connects, and moves everything through the cycles of life.

Everything Is Alive

ALL things in the physical world are endowed with living energy known as Ch'i. This includes the material possessions we may have considered inanimate, such as cars, computers, furniture, and appliances; as well as rocks, plants, land, and buildings. Every single physical thing is "alive" and endowed with its own unique Ch'i qualities, as well as the Ch'i qualities we bring to it with our own reactions, experiences, and memories. When our personal responses blend harmoniously with the things around us, we feel a deep sense of harmony, comfort, and safety. Obviously, when we look around and see everything surrounding us as being "alive," it becomes vastly more important to live with things we feel good about.

In Feng Shui, buildings are viewed as dynamic, living "bodies" with one purpose—to totally support and nurture their inhabitants. Their Ch'i is ideally very harmonious and nurturing to people, and their embrace is quite literal. Anything less needs immediate correction to assure the safety, comfort, and happiness of those who live or work there. Homes and workplaces are serving their purpose when they are experienced as safe harbors, powerful springboards, comfortable nests, and personal paradises by the inhabitants.

"One person's junk is another person's treasure" is a common saying that relates to the "aliveness" your thoughts and memories can give to an object. A joyful memory attached to the simplest object can empower it with vital Ch'i that feeds you every time you look at it. A pine cone or a feather picked up during a vision quest, a china teacup that Grandma used to serve you hot cocoa in, a faded photograph of you and your best friend at the age of six—these are examples of objects imbued with special aliveness by the happy emotions you feel every time you see them.

Items that have unhappy memories or feelings attached to them, or that you simply don't like, do not carry the living vital Ch'i that is supportive of you. The fastest way to transform the aliveness of these objects into something that is fresh and wholesome is to let them go. Sell, throw, or give them away! Your junk is put back into the flow, and may very well become another person's treasure. The Ch'i has an opportunity to be recharged or recycled, while you enjoy the lightness of being that comes with lightening your baggage and surrounding yourself with things that have positive, happy associations.

Everything Is Connected

Ch'i connects every physical thing. We live in an interconnected web of life, where everything is related to every other thing. Throw a pebble in a pond, and watch the whole pond be affected by the ripples of one small stone. This gives a special importance to your neighborhood and community, because the Ch'i flowing through them is also flowing, relatively undiluted, through your home or workplace.

The principle of interconnection continues indoors. For instance, the chaotic Ch'i in a crowded closet ripples out through the rest of a house and can have a restrictive effect on the whole space. The soothing, nurturing Ch'i generated by a beautiful atrium pulses through the surrounding area and can have a vibrantly positive effect on it. What's more, the Ch'i qualities of the closet or the atrium are connected to the rest of our lives. For instance, if the crowded, chaotic closet was in your home, it could affect your punctuality, which could undermine your receiving a promotion at work—which could produce financial stress, marital difficulties, and health disorders. Things that appear small and insignificant—an uncomfortable chair, a harsh light, a table with sharp corners—can have a major impact on your vital Ch'i when you are habitually connected to them. On the other hand, if the beautiful atrium was in your workplace, it could positively affect your health and enhance your relationships, as well as boost your creativity and financial gains. For better or worse, Ch'i connects you to everything, making all things in your life important.

Everything Is Changing

The Ch'i in everything is constantly changing. Growth and movement produce change and are the dynamic signs of vital, living Ch'i. The one thing that is constant in our physical universe is change.

We witness change everywhere we look—the seasons, our communities, our bodies, our states of mind, and our emotions. Therefore, our environments are not only alive and connected with their greater surroundings, they are also constantly changing. Along with the obvious physical changes homes and workplaces go through as time passes, they also reflect their inhabitants' changes.

In my Feng Shui practice, I've noticed that when people return home from a vacation, seminar, or retreat, or when they are packing for a move, they find that they suddenly want to change or discard certain things in their environment. The changes they've experienced give them a fresh perspective that acts like a laser beam, shedding light on anything that is no longer useful or energizing in their home or office. A worn piece of furniture, a crowded bookshelf, an overgrown tree, or a painting that's associated with an unhappy time, will suddenly "cry out" for change. By trusting their new perspective and making the changes that they can clearly see need to be made, these individuals are inviting fresh, harmonious Ch'i into their surroundings. What's more, they are literally anchoring the positive changes they've experienced so that their "new self" is constantly supported and nourished by their new environment.

It's interesting to note that an environment can actually pull a person back into old patterns if no changes are made in the home or workplace that reflect the changes the person has undergone. The environment acts like a huge magnet or anchor, holding the old thought patterns and experiences solidly in place. Consider the woman who spends a week at a health retreat to learn new cooking and eating habits. When she returns home, she realizes that her kitchen needs to be rearranged to match her new way of relating to food. If she leaves her kitchen exactly as it was before her retreat, she will be tempted to return to her old way of eating. If she changes the kitchen so that it anchors and supports her newly acquired knowledge, she will have a much easier time staying with the program.

There is a Chinese saying: "If you want change in your life, move 27 things in your house." The point here is to anchor your newest self in your environment by changing it to fit who you are now and who you want to be. Change is an integral part of life, and can be used to your advantage.

And, change can be playful, too. Many people pick out furniture that's supposed to last forever, choose art to match it, and figure that's it for life. Feng Shui suggests that they lighten up and begin to let their environments change, grow, move, and dance with the moment. Be fanciful, funny, fantastic, freaky, fabulous. Remember: it's all going to change, anyway!

▼▼▼

Chinese Symbol for Ch'i

Alive, connected, and dynamic...Feng Shui views your home or workplace as a living entity that you are either in harmony with or in discordant partnership with. When you honor its aliveness, recognize its vital connection with the quality of your entire life, and make the changes that keep it fresh and alive, it remains a delightful place to be. It nurtures, protects, and supports your growth and movement through life.

▼▼▼ ▼▼▼

Cease seeing with the mind,
and see with the vital spirit.

–Chuang Tzu

3

OPENING YOUR
FENG SHUI EYES

In this living, interconnected, dynamic "Sea of Ch'i," you can continually choose to surround yourself with the Ch'i that supports and nourishes your life. You have probably noticed that not just any Ch'i does this. Imagine eating your lunch in a crowded, windowless room that's too chilly, sitting on a hard chair pulled up to a table piled with papers and dirty dishes. Now, imagine eating the same lunch in a warm and spacious room with a nice view, seated in a comfortable chair at a table appointed with a candle and a colorful flower arrangement. Which room has the Ch'i in which you'd like to spend your time?

Most of us have a large appetite for the Ch'i inherent in beauty, comfort, and safety. And, many of us are starving for it. Our culture is riddled with "putting up with" on a daily basis—working or living in unaesthetic, uncomfortable, and unsafe environments. I believe that we endure these conditions because we don't realize how our environments can negatively impact our lives. We believe that our lives are compartmentalized, divided into parts that don't necessarily relate to one another.

Feng Shui is about wholeness, not parts. Everything is alive, connected, and changing all the time. Your intuitive sensibility will tell you that the office with a low ceiling, buzzing fluorescent lights, and a cramped desk backed into a wall will impact every aspect of your life.

What to do in this case? Feng Shui says to do everything in your power to turn this space into an office that has a spacious work area facing the door, with proper lighting, and a fabulous chair. Balance and direct the Ch'i to achieve dynamic harmony—that's the purpose of Feng Shui.

Ch'i expresses itself in countless ways through everything that surrounds you. Pay close attention to exactly how the Ch'i is being expressed in your environment, and you will train yourself to "read the Ch'i," a skill that's required in order to work with the principles of Feng Shui.

Yin and Yang

The Ch'i that nourishes us, which Feng Shui concentrates on enhancing, is always striking a balance between two extremes. Ancients called these two extremes *yin* and *yang* (see list, page 16), and attached myriad associations to these properties. Yin relates to qualities such as feminine, back, dark, cool, soft, wet, earth, moon, and so on, while yang is associated with qualities such as masculine, front, light, hot, hard, dry, sky, and sun. Most of us prefer the "middle road," or a perfect mix of these yin and yang qualities.

When dramatic architecture and design becomes an expression of extremes, it can result in a Feng Shui nightmare. Sharp angles, radical proportions, and exaggerated forms may be viewed as fabulous artistic features, but they usually do not make cozy habitats for humans. The more extremely yin or yang the design is, the more unsuitable it will be for people to live or work in. An example of an extremely yin room is one that's dark and cavelike, with black furniture, dim lighting, and a low ceiling. A very yang room would be quite large, with a high ceiling

and windows that bake the room with sun—a living space that is fur-
nished sparingly with angular furniture and tables. To balance the
extremely yin room, we add yang components, such as brighter lights
and warm pastel colors. To balance the very yang room, we mix in yin
components, such as soft, upholstered furniture, rounded window treatments, and dark, rich colors. When yin and yang qualities are mixed
together just right, a human comfort zone emerges.

Generally speaking, humans are lovers of balanced yin and yang
expressions. We will instinctively place ourselves where things are
"just right" whenever we can. When we focus on establishing balance and harmony in our environments, a certain human-friendly
beauty is born.

What about your individual tastes? You may absolutely love and
cherish your 30-foot-high ceiling, huge white room, or sun-drenched
front office. These are great examples of your individual tastes being
more in the yang category. Or, you may glean tremendous comfort from
your basement nook, your dark and womblike den, or your tiny floral
bedroom. You wouldn't change a thing about them. Here, your tastes
lean toward the yin qualities. Gathering around you the things you love
is an expression of your own individual Ch'i. No matter how much you
break down and label things as yin or yang, it is essential to honor your
preferences, style, and opinions when you are creating your individual
personal paradise. When your ultimate goal is to live a life surrounded
by the things that turn you on, it doesn't matter if it ends up being
labeled lacy, stark, country, deco, eclectic, or contemporary. What mat-
ters is that it is a joyful expression of you.

Exercise:

Take a moment to look at how the Ch'i is expressing
itself in the room you are in now. Do you like what you
see, and do you feel absolutely comfortable there?
Using the yin/yang list on page 16, find the yin and the
yang features that make up the room. Determine
whether yin or yang qualities dominate, or if there is a

fairly even mix. This way of using your Feng Shui eyes can help you pinpoint exactly what the room may need to bring it into the perfect comfort zone.

If you like the room, you now know the approximate ratio of yin and yang that makes up your particular comfort zone, and you can arrange your other rooms accordingly.

FENG SHUI LIST OF
YIN AND YANG ASSOCIATIONS

YIN	YANG
Feminine	Masculine
Cool/Cold	Warm/Hot
Dark	Light
Back	Front
Soft	Hard
Curved	Straight
Rounded	Angular
Earth	Sky
Moon	Sun
Low	High
Small	Large
Ornate	Plain
Wide	Narrow
Horizontal	Vertical
Floral	Geometrical

The Five Elements Applied to Feng Shui

Now that your Feng Shui eyes know how to see the expressions of yin and yang, let's explore the five elements as they relate to our environment. These elements are: Wood, Fire, Earth, Metal, and Water, and they are considered the building blocks of everything physical on earth. Born out of the polaric interplay of yin and yang, the five elements manifest in countless ways and combinations around us. Feng Shui observes that human beings are made up of a combination of all five elements, and therefore are typically most comfortable when all of the elements are represented in their homes and workplaces. Although there are myriad elemental associations having to do with every aspect of life, we will focus on descriptions of the five elements that relate to our homes and workplaces.

There are three skills we develop and use when working with the five elements:

1. Defining the elements in an environment
2. Assessing the need for elemental additions and corrections
3. Making specific recommendations to establish elemental balance

The ability to define, assess, and balance the elements reveals (to the practiced eye) exactly what needs to be done in order to bring an environment into perfect elemental balance. It is one of the potent tools in Feng Shui that shows us where to tap to produce a positive result. Before I learned to see the elements, I could tell when an environment was out of balance, but I didn't know exactly why, and I didn't know exactly what to do about it. Now, the elements tell me what to do to achieve balance.

Each of the five elements has a rich spectrum of associations—including colors, shapes, and qualities—that form the language for observing and directing their expression. And, the elements are constantly combining, as described under "Elemental Combinations" on page 21. The fastest and easiest way to learn this language is to practice defining your own environment in elemental terms. At first, seeing the expression of the elements may seem foreign to you. But, if you practice, you will soon be fluent and able to describe the dance of the elements everywhere you go.

Exercise:

Begin with the room you are sitting in now. Use the "Five Elements Worksheet" on the next page and the elements lists on pages 20 and 21. Look for:

1. **The actual elements themselves**: Wood, Fire, Earth, Metal, and Water.

2. **Things made out of the elements**, such as wooden furniture representing the Wood element.

3. **Things that represent the elements**, such as rocks relating to the Metal element, or mirrors representing the Water element.

4. **Artwork that depicts the elements**, such as landscape paintings representing the Wood element, or sculptures of animals representing the Fire element.

5. **Things that are in the associated color and/or shape of the elements**, such as a red chair, signifying Fire, or a square table representing Earth.

THE FIVE ELEMENTS
Worksheet

Date:

Room:

☐ Earth:

◎ Metal:

Water:

Wood:

△ Fire:

Elemental Combinations:

Suggestions:

THE WOOD ELEMENT is found in:

- Wooden furniture and accessories
- Wooden paneling, siding, roofing, and decks
- All indoor and outdoor plants and flowers, including silk, plastic, and dried material
- All types of plant-based cloth and textiles, such as cotton and rayon
- Floral print upholstery, wall coverings, draperies, and linens
- Art depicting landscapes, gardens, plants, and flowers
- The columnar shape, like the trunk of a tree, found in columns, beams, pedestals, poles, and stripes
- The green and blue spectrum of colors

THE FIRE ELEMENT is found in:

- All lighting, including electric, oil, candles, natural sunlight, and fireplaces (see "Lighting" on page 159)
- Things made from animals, such as fur, leather, bone, feathers, and wool
- Pets and wildlife
- Art that depicts people and/or animals
- Art that depicts sunshine, light, or fire
- Shapes such as triangles, pyramids, or cones
- The red spectrum of colors

THE EARTH ELEMENT is found in:

- Adobe, brick, and tile
- Ceramic or earthenware objects
- Shapes such as squares, rectangles, and long, flat surfaces
- The yellow and earth-tone spectrum of colors
- Art depicting earthy landscapes of desert, fields, and so on

THE METAL ELEMENT is found in:

- All types of metals, including stainless steel, copper, brass, iron, silver, aluminum, and gold
- All rocks and stones, such as marble, granite, and flagstone
- Natural crystals, rocks, and gemstones
- Art and sculpture made from metal or stone
- The white and light pastel spectrum of colors
- The shapes of the circle, oval, and arch

THE WATER ELEMENT is found in:

- Streams, rivers, pools, fountains, and water features of all kinds (see "Water Features" on page 164)
- Reflective surfaces, such as cut crystal, glass, and mirrors
- Flowing, free-form, and asymmetrical shapes
- The black and dark-tone spectrum of colors, such as charcoal gray and midnight blue.

Elemental Combinations

It's interesting to notice the elemental combinations in the things around you. An aquarium, classically used in Feng Shui to enhance the Ch'i, is a great example of all five elements joined together in one expression. The water itself, along with the glass container, represents the Water element; the plants express the Wood element; the fish symbolize the Fire element; the sand represents the Earth element; and the rocks symbolize the Metal element. Think of your favorite natural paradise, and you will probably notice that it's made up of a harmonious blend of all five elements, whether it's on an island, in the mountains, or deep in a forest.

At home and at work, you can create five-element arrangements in an infinite variety. Think of all the different combinations you can put together by using the things, colors, and shapes associated with each element. For instance, in front of a mirror (representing the Water element), you could place a healthy plant (representing Wood), in a red terra cotta pot (symbolizing Fire and Earth). To bring in the Metal element, you could then place a polished rock or small bronze statue with the plant, and you have all five elements collected together in a simple five-element arrangement.

Elemental Expression

The elements combine in innumerable ways to create physical forms. One of the easiest ways to work with the five elements in your environment is to observe which ones are missing—on a table, in a room, in a house, on a piece of land—and add them. This is done in the spirit of harmony, using things you love. As you know, the most simple item can be a mix of several elements. Let's use a table in my office as an example. When I analyze its elemental composition, I see that the table is a blend of three of the elements. It is rectangular (Earth), black (Water), and painted with flowers (Wood). To bring the other two elements in, I have added a round white coaster (Metal), and a lamp (Fire). This arrangement harmoniously joins all five elements, lifting and enhancing the Ch'i in the room.

In working with the five elements, you are training yourself in a whole new way of seeing. Take your time and relax while you're practicing. It's possible to elementally pick things apart to the point of driving yourself crazy. That's not the objective of these observations. Defining the overall elemental composition of an item or environment is all that is necessary to be able to achieve the desired result—elemental balance.

Exercise:

Look around where you are right now, and choose a piece of furniture such as a table, bureau, or credenza.

Break it down elementally, and see what elements you have. If one or more of the elements are missing, decide how you can introduce them. When you have brought all five elements together in a harmonious arrangement, pay attention to whether you can actually feel the Ch'i strengthen and balance around you.

Now, define the room where you are sitting in elemental terms. Suspend your usual way of looking at the room, as well as thoughts about whether you like the room or not, and simply make a list of the elements that surround you in the room. After you're done, notice whether there is a dominant element. Also, see if there is a missing element(s). Contemplate how you could add any missing elements.

The Nourishing and Controlling Cycles of the Five Elements

In the Nourishing Cycle of the five elements (see the chart on page 24), each element feeds and sustains the other in perfect harmony:

- Water nurtures Wood,
- Wood feeds Fire,
- Fire makes Earth,
- Earth creates Metal, and
- Metal holds Water.

The Nourishing Cycle shows us how the elements strengthen and feed each other in an endless regenerating cycle. When all five elements are present in an environment, a natural balance is achieved.

In the Controlling Cycle, we see how the elements can dominate and control each other:

- Wood consumes Earth,
- Earth dams Water,
- Water extinguishes Fire,
- Fire melts Metal, and
- Metal cuts Wood.

It's important to remember that the Controlling Cycle of the elements is not a negative influence. Rather, it can be one of the most appealing ways to achieve elemental harmony, and is present in many of the places we consider the most beautiful.

THE FIVE ELEMENTS
Nourishing and Controlling Relationships

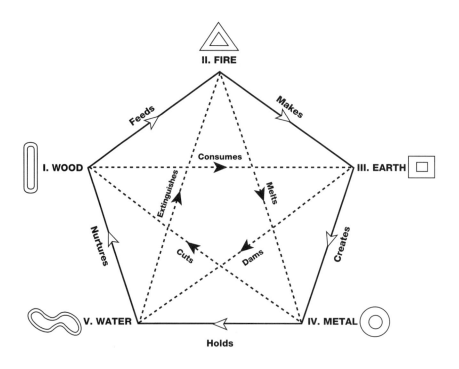

Nourishing ————
Controlling - - - - - - - -

Imagine walking across a desert, earth stretching out as far as the eye can see. Then, on the horizon, you catch a glimpse of a stand of ancient trees, their leafy branches reaching up to the sky. This is Wood (the trees) "consuming" Earth (the desert). Imagine hiking through a deep forest, a wood landscape made up of endless plants and trees. Then, around a bend, you come upon a family of boulders, colored with lichen and scored with countless veins, set in among the trees. This is Metal (the rocks) "cutting" Wood (the trees). Or, think about looking out over the infinite blue ocean and seeing a golden sandy island shimmering in the distance. This is Earth (the island) "damming" Water (the ocean). Nature constantly provides us with examples of how the controlling cycle of the elements can create balance and beauty.

It is very useful to be aware of both the nourishing and the controlling cycles of the five elements when you're balancing the elemental Ch'i of an environment. When one element is especially predominant, the controlling cycle will show you which element to introduce to quickly achieve balance. Once you have matched a dominant element with its controlling partner, you can turn to the nourishing cycle and further refine your elemental balance.

For instance, many homes I've worked with are dominated by the Wood element, including my own, which I will use as an example. My home is covered with wooden shingles, has a wooden front deck, and is surrounded by gardens and trees. Inside, it is wallpapered in floral prints, with lots of built-in wooden cabinets and detailing. It is wood, wood, wood!

When we moved in, I knew right away we didn't need house plants or an oak floor, both associated with the Wood element. What we needed was a strong dose of the Metal element—the controlling element of Wood—to elementally balance the house. We purchased cream couches with rounded arms and backs, pastel linens for the bedroom, and cream carpeting, all in Metal's domain. We had a collection of bronze lamps and natural rocks—both representing the Metal element—to place around the house. I also replaced the large floral tile in our coffee table with plain white marble to bring in both the color and stone associations of the Metal element. To strengthen the Metal presence even more, I made sure that the Earth element, which nourishes Metal, was highlighted. This was done by placing a large golden yellow candle on the coffee table. This highlight also brought in the Fire element. Since Wood feeds Fire, the candle symbolically helped to "burn" the over-abundance of wood in the house.

The existing brick fireplace also represented both Fire and Earth. When the fireplace is not in use during the summer months, I make it into a rock garden using sand (Earth) and several rounded light-colored rocks (Metal). Except for the large mirror over the fireplace, I was careful not to bring in much of the Water element, because in the nourishing cycle, Water feeds Wood. Given the existing "woody" environment, it would have been a mistake to have put dark couches, linens, or carpet in the house, due to their association with the Water element. Heavy use of mirrors, glass, or crystal would have presented a problem for the same reason.

When working with the Controlling Element Cycle, remember:

- If the dominating element is Wood, introduce the controlling element of Metal, and highlight with Earth and Fire. Do not use much Water.

- If the dominating element is Fire, introduce the controlling element of Water, and highlight with Metal and Earth. Do not use much Wood.

- If the dominating element is Earth, introduce the controlling element of Wood, and highlight with Metal and Water. Do not use much Fire.

- If the dominating element is Metal, introduce the controlling element of Fire, and highlight with Water and Wood. Do not use much Earth.

- If the dominating element is Water, introduce the controlling element of Earth, and highlight with Wood and Fire. Do not use much Metal.

Exercise:

Here's an interesting experiment for you to try. I'll describe the exercise first, then give an example.

Choose a room in your home or office where one element dominates. First, decide which element NOURISHES the dominant element by looking at the Nourishing Cycle Chart, then decide which element CONTROLS it by looking at the Controlling Cycle Chart. Now, find an object that represents the Nourishing element, and place it prominently in the room. Notice what it does to the Ch'i. Remove it, and bring in something that represents the controlling element. Place it prominently in the room. Pay attention to the changes in the Ch'i.

Using my living room as an example, the dominant element is Wood. Water is the element that feeds Wood. To accentuate the Water element, I drape dark cloths over the couches. This further feeds the Wood element, and I notice that the Ch'i in the room turns "swampy" and uninviting with so much dark Watery color feeding the already dominant Wood.

Next, I uncover the couches, whose light cream color represents metal, and I observe the difference. The swampy Ch'i disappears, and a comfortable, balanced feeling fills the room. Then, I add my Earth and Fire highlights to strengthen the elemental balance even more.

This experiment is a real Feng Shui eye-opener. Most people are struck by what a positive difference they can make in an environment by simply balancing a dominant element with its controlling partner and then adding elemental highlights. Call it Feng Shui alchemy. Mix the five elements just right, and you will have an environment of gold.

▼▼▼ ▼▼▼

Love thy neighbor as thyself,
but choose your neighborhood.

—*Louise Beal*

4

LOCATION, LOCATION, LOCATION

The title of this chapter is a popular phrase used by real estate professionals when they're explaining why a piece of property costs what it does. Location is everything in their world, and it is of key importance in the Feng Shui world as well. Some locations are auspicious by nature—they have all the right features in all the right places. But, most locations have some less-than-excellent aspects that need balancing.

Feng Shui also addresses the locations of features such as doors, windows, corners, beams, streets, and neighboring buildings. Each and every one of these features has an impact on your home and workplace—an impact you want to be sure is human-friendly.

It is my belief that there are very few hopeless cases. When your intent is focused on living in a balanced environment and you apply Feng Shui principles to achieve that result, you can successfully treat most environmental injuries and maladies. Environments respond the way people do to tender loving care. Even a small increase in the Ch'i can help bring about the changes necessary to move you to a more balanced structure.

Home Sweet Home

We know that ideal locations for homes are those that are somewhere between the mountaintops and the flood plains, with harmonious representations of all five elements around them. When this isn't what we have to work with, we look at how we can make it so. You can create the ideal "armchair" shape around your home by planting hedges and trees, adding berms, or installing fencing in the back and around the sides of the property. You can introduce water to the front of your property by placing a water feature of some kind there, or by creating a meandering path that reminds you of the flow of water. You can "cozy" yourself in, personalize your surroundings, and enhance the Ch'i by adding flower beds, vegetable gardens, patios, decks, grottoes, and viewing gardens. Accent with rock walls, boulders, and white flowers to bring in the Metal element. Add statuary of animals or people, and plant bright red flowers to highlight the Fire element. Introduce gold and yellow flowers to strengthen the Earth element. The possibilities are endless!

When you live in a condo without land of its own, or if the land around you is unworkable for some reason, apply the same principles indoors. Bring nature inside. The more urban the environment, the more important it is to bring the five elements in their natural form into your home. Bring in objects such as plants, flowers, rocks, shells, leather, wool, candles, and water. A small water feature in the front room of an apartment or home symbolizes flowing water in front of the property and provides harmonious sounds that mask urban noises. Large plants symbolize a protective forest in the back of the apartment, while window coverings protect the sides of your home.

The Streets Where We Live

In Feng Shui, streets are seen as "waterways," channeling Ch'i at a variety of speeds, from the raging rivers of interstate highways, to the meandering streams of country roads, to the stop-and-go quagmires of city intersections.

In many Western countries, there are large populations of people who live on or very near the raging rivers of beltways, interstates, and other heavily used highways. Large freeways are moving far too quickly to nourish the buildings, land, or people along their banks. Besides the obvious effect these locations may have on people's health, the raging Ch'i can pull on their property, "eroding" and carrying away the beneficial Ch'i.

The bigger and closer that busy roads are to your house, the more Ch'i builders and enhancers you'll need to establish a healthy balance. (Look at the chapter on Basic Feng Shui Tools beginning on page 157 for suggestions.) For instance, plants clean the air of toxins and can provide a visual screen, whether you plant an urban forest between your house and a highway, or line your condo balcony with potted plants. Water features and harmonious sound makers enliven an area with nourishing Ch'i and provide an auditory screen from traffic noise. Fences and walls are a beginning, but they need to be augmented with living or moving things to continually refresh the Ch'i.

Also challenging are cul-de-sacs and T-intersections. If we look at these configurations as waterways, we can see that the street stops, but the Ch'i keeps going like a tidal wave directly into the house in its path. This would be fine if tidal waves of Ch'i hitting the house were nourishing to us. However, for most people, it's too much to be healthy. A protective barrier between the street and the house, made of foliage, fencing, and other landscaping features, can be arranged around the front of the home. This barrier provides the needed protection from the onslaught of the Ch'i rolling in from the street, while supplying nourishing Ch'i directly to the house.

In general, when you look at roads as waterways, you can usually ascertain whether their Ch'i is human-friendly or not. As always, the more extreme a feature is—in this case, roads—the more likely it will need to be balanced to achieve comfort and harmony.

Our Windows and Doors

Ch'i flows in and out of buildings through the windows and doors. To "see" the primary flow of Ch'i through any building, look in through the front doorway. The windows and/or doors you can see from that vantage point show the primary path that the Ch'i takes. This is true with each room as well. Stand in the doorway, look through to the window(s) or other door(s), and there's your primary Ch'i path.

As always, we want a nice, friendly, meandering flow between door and window. The larger either feature is, the more likely it is that the Ch'i is moving too quickly to nourish the area on its way through. For instance, think of walking into an office and seeing huge floor-to-ceiling windows wrapped around two sides of the room. The view is "stunning" and could easily pull you across the room. You, and every bit of Ch'i that enters the door, are being yanked across and out those gaping, gorgeous squares of glass. As beautiful as it may be, it's problematic when it comes to keeping the Ch'i in the room for more than a few seconds. The person inhabiting the office is very likely experiencing Ch'i depletion in the form of an overwhelming workload, high stress levels, and relentless activity without much support. He or she is being "yanged" to death, so to speak. This is an example of an extremely yang architectural feature that needs to be balanced with yin influences so that the Ch'i entering the door has a chance to meander around and nourish the room before it travels out again. All it may take is the soft curve of drapes, low horizontal lines of cabinets in front of the windows, or an ornate corner arrangement of plants and sculpture to balance the yin and yang expressions of Ch'i and bring harmony into the room.

On the other hand, when a room has no windows to create a Ch'i path, it can feel stagnant or devoid of Ch'i. Many bathrooms and offices are built like this. Yang influences such as large mirrors to enlarge the space, and lots of Ch'i-enhancers, such as flowers, bright colors, lights, and nature objects, help to attract more Ch'i into the room.

Anytime a window or a door is located directly across from another window or door, there is the tendency for the Ch'i to stream too quickly through the space in between. If you open your front door, and you can see your back door or a window directly in front of you through the house, you're seeing a Ch'i path that's probably moving too quickly to nourish its surroundings. When at all possible, place something such as a screen, furniture, plants, or art in between to slow the Ch'i down and guide it out to other parts of the house. Just like our bodies' digestive systems, to be well nourished by the Ch'i in our surroundings, we require that the Ch'i in our environments move neither too fast nor too slow, but just right.

Other People's Windows and Doors

We all enjoy a sense of privacy, and in Feng Shui, privacy is a top priority because of the negative effects of the lack of it. Our living and working environments are our personal domains, and for us to feel that they are our paradises means that they need to feel private. Many of our suburban and city dwellings are built cheek by jowl, and from every window and door we can see the windows and doors of other buildings. As part of setting up our ideal location, we need to artfully bring privacy to our residence, and often to our office areas as well.

Our relationships with our neighbors, whether they're in the next cubicle or the next house, are much more harmonious when we feel we are not being looked in on day and night. I have been in many homes where the occupants are waiting for the trees to grow to gain a sense of privacy. Their relationships with their neighbors are usually strained because everyone is feeling too close for comfort. As we know, the Ch'i circulating around our neighborhood is affecting our health and happiness all the time. So, it's best that we cultivate workable relationships with our neighbors while making sure the views from their windows and doors are kept where they belong—well outside our private domains.

The most obvious way to bring privacy to your space is to install coverings, especially on windows and doors where other windows and doors are "looking in." When a neighboring window or door is especially invasive, such as when their front door is directly across from yours, a small mirror can be hung outside facing the offending door, thereby sending the invasive Ch'i back to its origin. Plants that are hung or placed at just the right height can do the privatizing trick, along with screens, fencing, and well-placed art objects. The point is to make sure you don't feel like someone can see you by simply looking in your direction.

Offices and Workplaces

The cloistered little "belly of the dragon"—a safe location sheltered from the world—is not necessarily the ideal business location. Here we prefer the "eye" of the dragon—out in front, clear and focused, ready to direct the show. When a place to conduct business is being chosen, it is common knowledge that a prominent location and advertising are two crucial components for success. Still, there are many businesses that end up being located back in the "tail" of the dragon, so to speak. The less visible your business is to the public, the more you need to strengthen and power up the Ch'i in order to direct business your way.

The artful use of the Basic Feng Shui Tools (see page 155) can be applied to businesses as well as to residences. Do not underestimate the power of bright flags; banners; sound makers such as bells, music, and water; and colorful samples of the store's goods waving in the breeze to attract customers. I have found that banners displaying bright store colors, symbols, and/or logos are especially eye-catching and lend an air of celebration that appeals to customers. These devices act like giant, friendly hands beckoning people to come in and enjoy themselves. Wind chimes, bells, and music are other choices for literally reaching out to people as they pass by. It's especially important to balance the Ch'i of a recessed location by "reaching out" from your place of business with color, motion, and flair.

Such was the case with a wholesale florist who was also open to the public. Her warehouse location had an entrance that couldn't be seen from the street, and zoning restrictions prohibited large signs. However, by applying Feng Shui principles, I realized that this business could "reach out" and attract people in a colorful, creative way. By painting a brightly hued garland of flowers along the side of the building, customers were beckoned to, and guided around the building and into the florist's entrance.

I also suggested that the business move its cash register to enhance the Ch'i of wealth and prosperity (see the Bagua Map on page 62), reposition the work tables to enhance the flow of customer traffic, and set up a prominent display of vases to expand the inventory of retail items and add interest to the store. The attractive garland of painted flowers and the interior Feng Shui balancing and enhancements did the trick. Customers poured in, buying armloads of fresh flowers and supplies, while the owner of the floral warehouse enjoyed a booming business.

Prominently located businesses, on the other hand, need to attract customers by enhancing the Ch'i inside. As people pass by and look into such an establishment, they can be irresistibly drawn in if something catches their eyes. For example, a large optical company asked for Feng Shui assistance during their remodeling project. I suggested that they put up a brightly colored banner across the back wall that displayed the company name. When people took a peek in as they passed by, they were drawn into the store by the festive colors beckoning from that back wall.

I have worked with many stores and businesses that make the same mistake. They plaster their windows full of signs, information, and photographs of goods and services that block the view inside. This is common in smaller businesses, such as those marketing medical services, health and gourmet foods, and specialty items. Instead of being attracted to something wonderful inside the store, one of two things happens to people instead. They either pause to look at the information, find out what they need to know, and then continue on their way, or they're turned off by the onslaught of visual information inflicted upon them and (more quickly) continue on their way. Obviously, neither option is good for business. While the owners think they're performing a service to post interesting news and information in the windows, they are actually doing both themselves and their customers a great disservice.

I recently worked with a medical office that had an excellent location. As I approached their front entrance, I counted 14 different items in the window. There was enough reading material to keep someone busy for 15 minutes. I suggested that they simplify their windows by removing everything except the sign stating their hours. This modification opened the view to their waiting area, which we rearranged to be inviting and comfortable. A bulletin board on an interior wall provided patients with reading material in the waiting area, and was also an appealing point of interest when seen from the window. After these changes, the receptionist noticed that more people came in, inquired about their services, and made appointments to see the doctor.

If you are a business owner, take a Feng Shui look at your location. If you are secluded or off the beaten path in any way, you need to do something special on the outside to attract customers. If you are in a prominent location, you need to concentrate on drawing people into the heart of the store by doing something special on the inside. People will thank you for making these changes by bringing you their business.

Once inside an establishment, many Feng Shui principles described throughout this book can come into play. Furnishings, displays, and counters are ideally set up with a minimum of corners pointed toward the customers and employees. Wide pathways meander invitingly through the merchandise. The five elements are represented in perfect balance, creating an environment that people want to bask in—and spend their money in. The Bagua areas (see the Bagua Map on page 62) of the store are set up to the owner's advantage. The cash register is placed in an auspicious location, usually either in the Wealth area of the store, or in the Wealth area of the sales counter. Missing Bagua areas are balanced with mirrors or other Feng Shui tools; and ceilings, beams, and stairways are balanced to achieve environmental harmony—boosting sales, customer satisfaction, and repeat business.

▼▼▼ ▼▼▼

Do what you can,
with what you have,
with where you are.

—*Theodore Roosevelt*

5

BALANCING STRUCTURAL
FEATURES

The Ch'i that nourishes us is balanced between extremes. In a harmonious environment, Ch'i meanders in, flows around in the buoyant, refreshing manner of a spring breeze, and then meanders out again. With our Feng Shui eyes open, we now take on the job of smoothing out all the rough edges that curtail or prevent this nourishing flow from occurring.

We want to undertake this task because of the insidious nature of unfriendly Ch'i in our environments. We can be in an unbalanced environment for an hour, a day, or perhaps even a week and maintain our inner balance. But if we live or work there day after day, month after month, it begins to wear away at us like water dripping on a stone.

There is a classic story that illustrates this dilemma: A man has to stoop under an overgrown branch to get in his front door. He does not trim the branch and has to stoop every day for a year to get in his door. Soon, he begins to walk in a stooped posture everywhere he goes. One branch in need of a trim has changed this man's gait. His stoop leads to illness, loss of work, and financial problems.

Now, the man's neighbor comes to the door with fresh vegetables from his garden. The branch hinders the neighbor's easy access to the door, so instead of putting his basket down and stooping to get to the door, he decides to take his produce to someone else. What's more, the neighbor leaves with the impression that the man isn't very friendly. Why would he let the branch grow in front of his door if he were? He decides that he won't visit the man again. In the days that follow, the neighbor mentions his experience to several people. Each time the story is told, it gets more exaggerated, with everyone concluding that the man is an embarrassment to the neighborhood because of his poorly kept property and unwelcoming demeanor. The compounded impact of one seemingly insignificant thing in the man's life has become great indeed.

People make snap decisions all the time depending on how they feel when they approach a person or a building. The branch was just enough to change the neighbor's mind about giving his gift, leaving him with negative impressions that he then shared with others. When we view this story in the context of how clients, customers, and helpful people of all kinds feel when they enter our home and work environments, we can understand how important it is to roll out the welcome mat and clear the way!

The Mouths of Ch'i—Thresholds

How many thresholds do we cross over each day? Each one is considered a "mouth" through which Ch'i, like breath, enters and departs. In Feng Shui, the front entrance is the largest and most important mouth of Ch'i. It represents our relationship with society and is meant to welcome and direct positive, vital Ch'i in the form of energy, people, and opportunities into a building. A distinct path leading to the front entrance from the street or sidewalk helps to identify its importance and channel nourishing Ch'i to it.

Ideally, all thresholds are kept clear of anything that would hinder the door from fully opening. After all, we want to invite all the nourishing Ch'i we can to come in, and we certainly want the people entering there to feel welcome and comfortable. I have visited many homes and offices where there's something behind the doors, preventing them from opening fully. This hindrance creates a reduction in the Ch'i flow, as well as provoking a reaction of annoyance and irritation each time a person tries to open the door. When doors are allowed to open fully, the people walking through them can open fully to promising opportunities, resources, and circumstances in their lives. The way is clear for positive things to happen. Also, thresholds ought to be kept clear of wires, cords, toys, and any other object that produces a feeling of caution. These "booby traps" negatively affect the Ch'i, are unsafe, and rile, rather than soothe, occupants and visitors.

The goal is for thresholds to usher you from one comfortable space into another. When a wall appears to be "in your face" as you walk through a door, it's probably too close for comfort. The rule of thumb is that there should be a minimum of six feet between a door and a wall, and for many people, that's still too close. Mirrors are often the perfect treatment for a wall that's lording over a door. Another good choice is art that has a three-dimensional quality, such as a landscape or oceanscape.

Walls that are partially in view when entering a room can be just as unnerving. What you see is a wall that's close on one side of your visual field, and an extended view into a room on the other side. This split in the view is commonly found in foyers and bedrooms, and can be very disconcerting to the brain and the nervous system. Balance this feature as you would a wall that's too close. Use a mirror (large enough to reflect at least your entire head), or art that has a three-dimensional quality.

Exercise

Put something behind the front door of your home so that it's partially blocked from opening, and then exit and enter through the door several times. Be aware of how you feel when you cannot fully open the door.

Now remove the obstacle to open the way fully, and enter and exit several times. Notice the difference.

Threshold of the Automobile—Garages

Many of my residential clients live in homes in which the attached garage juts out in front of the rest of the house toward the street. As convenient as that sounds, this location exalts the garage's importance and gives great power to its mechanical inhabitant, the automobile. In many cases, the front door of the house is recessed back from the garage and dwarfed by the huge "mouth" of the garage doors. This communicates that the car is more important than the people. The automobile becomes the ruling force—a perfect example of a great servant becoming an unfortunate master. It's no wonder that the people who live in garage-dominated houses often complain of too much stress and activity in their lives, of hurriedly driving from one event to another, and of "living" in their cars, not in their homes.

Their structural problem is compounded when the garage is in constant chaos. Think about how often you are in and out of your garage. You are being influenced by what you see there as much as by what surrounds you in any other room in your house. Coming and going from a place that is disorganized, crowded, and chaotic can become a metaphor for your life.

Here are some things you can do to offset these potential problems:

- When building your own home, consider locating your garage in its own building at the back or side of the house or property. When it is included under the same roof as the house, it is best for it to be hidden from the front entrance without changing the overall shape of the house itself.

- The threshold, or front door, of your home is very important, as it represents your relationship with society. When your front entrance is structurally recessed back from the garage, it's important to literally or symbolically bring it forward. You can do this with artful landscaping, room additions, lighting, arbors, decks, patios, porches, fencing, or walls. Any entrance can be made more prominent by enhancing and beautifying the approach to it and the area around it. The idea is to make your front entrance so inviting and attractive that it draws attention away from the garage door and puts the focus on the all-important front door.

- When possible, shroud the garage door with screening, landscaping, or fencing so that it is not so prominently visible from the street.

- Paint your garage the same color as the house, and keep it free of decorations that draw attention to it.

- Organize and enhance the garage itself. In Feng Shui, the garage is as important as any other room in the house. Make it beautiful! You can carpet it, organize it, beautify it, and enhance it in any number of ways. One of my clients has a particularly inviting garage. She laid down some of the wall-to-wall carpeting she'd replaced inside her home, added posters of beautiful nature scenes, and installed shelves along the sides to organize her garden supplies. Now when she drives into her garage, she is greeted by a soft, quiet, organized space. She feels welcome from the very second she drives through the garage door.

- If you enter and exit your home through an interior garage door rather than the front door to the house, make sure to beautify and enhance that entrance as well. Give yourself the same inviting experience that you provide for the people who enter through your front door. It doesn't matter if it's a laundry room, store room, or back hall, it can be transformed into a small art gallery, a portrait studio, or a place to display a collection of things you love. What's important is to make it wonderful, well lit, and easily accessible.

Relaxation, rejuvenation, and recreation are three primary functions of a home. The garage can act as a call to constant action, scraping away daily at the very reasons a home exists. Your garage needs to be "put in its place" if your home is to be a place of peace.

Setting the Stage—First Impressions

The room you enter first when you walk into a building is the one that sets the stage for the entire place. Foyers, living rooms, and lobbies are the classic entry rooms, welcoming people and giving them a chance to settle into the environment before they go into another room.

When the room entered initially is a kitchen, dining room, office, or bedroom, those areas will also suggest what the focus of the house is. For example, kitchens and dining rooms will bring to mind food and eating, so that guests tend to notice right away how hungry they are and how nice it would be to stay for dinner.

A couple I recently worked with had actually rerouted their front walkway to bring guests in through the kitchen. I asked them if they enjoyed feeding people, and they both lit up with big smiles. Yes! Their house was a place where large community potlucks were held two or three times a week. Their home's entrance served them in a perfect, if slightly unconventional, way.

On the other hand, I worked with a woman who was finding it very difficult to overcome bulimia. As it turned out, her front door opened directly into the dining room. We were able to move her dining table and chairs to a kitchen nook and transform the room intended to be a dining room into a large atrium. Her front door now opens to a beautiful indoor garden, filled with large palms, flowering bromeliads, and a natural rock water feature. With the furniture that symbolized eating out of sight, and the Ch'i-enhancing qualities of the plants and the water there to greet her, she noticed immediately how much easier it was to correct and balance her eating habits.

Studio apartments often present the challenge of walking directly into a bedroom setting. Bedrooms have many associations, from sleepy to suggestive, and are best located away from the front entrance.

Therefore it's a good idea to either screen the bed from the entrance, or choose a bed that can be put away, such as a futon or Murphy bed.

Obviously, direct entry into an office will set the stage for work, work, work. This may be exactly what you want; however, people usually appreciate being given a moment to arrive and settle themselves into an environment before they move on to the next task. Depending on the amount of space you have, a welcoming "pause" may be achieved in many ways, such as placing a water station near the door, providing an area to sit before getting to one's desk, or having a full-fledged lobby where people can catch their breath before leaping into the work mode.

Front and Back—Room Location

The most active Ch'i is found in the rooms that are located in the front of a building. When that room is the garage, then the garage will be the most active. When it's the living room in a home, or the offices in a workplace, then they are the most active, and the space strikes a harmoniously functional chord.

What often doesn't work well is to have a bedroom in the front of the house, or an office or studio in the back. Likewise, to place the most active work stations at the back of an office building goes against the natural Ch'i flow.

Bedrooms, and the rooms located back and away from the front entrance, are considered yin areas. They work well as places for deep relaxation, retreat, and rejuvenation. Awake rooms such as living, kitchen, and work rooms are considered yang, as is the front of the house. They also work well together. When a bedroom is located in the front of the house, sleep is often interrupted or negatively affected by the abundance of yang Ch'i there. The active feeling of the front of a building can be purely energetic, or it can be actually bombarded by the "awake" sounds of streets, people, and so on. Conversely, an office or living room located in the back recesses of a home, office building, or business complex can suffer from a chronic lack of active, awake Ch'i, draining the people trying to work or entertain there.

When possible, simply locate the bedrooms in the back of the house. I have worked with several homes where we turned the master bedroom suite, in all its front-of-the-house glory, into an office or studio. A room in the back of the house was then made into the bedroom. This can be a surprisingly satisfying solution. Bedrooms serve us best when they are cozy. The larger a bedroom is, the more yang it is, often lacking the intimate feeling that nourishes our sleep and lovemaking.

When it is not possible to move a bedroom to the back of the house, there are still many Feng Shui adjustments you can make. To balance the yang location, such as a bedroom in the front of the house, bring yin influences in such as dark, rich colors, prints and horizontal stripes, as well as soft, overstuffed furniture, and low lighting (see the Yin-Yang list, page 16). Be sure that the five elements are also represented in the room.

As for offices delegated to the back of a home or office building, Feng Shui balances the yin Ch'i with yang influences. Bright lights, white, pastel, and bright colors, and angular lines in the furniture are a few examples of introducing more items of the yang persuasion. Along with these, the addition of a cheery interior water feature, upbeat music, and other Ch'i enhancers such as wind chimes, flags, or banners will activate and circulate the Ch'i, balancing the yin and yang energies.

Breaking the Mold—Room Usage

Our homes and office buildings were built with specific uses for each room in mind. They are named by builders and architects as the Living Room, the Dining Room, the Master Bedroom, the President's Office, the Storeroom, and so on. However, if any of these rooms do not serve us well, their function needs to be questioned. Is the master bedroom or the living room better used as an art or dance studio? Does the guest room or formal dining room really need to be changed into a much-needed office? Does the largest office really work as one person's space, or is it best used as an employee lounge? Guest rooms can be changed into offices, bedrooms into studios, studios into bedrooms, storerooms into offices, conference rooms into lounges, dens into dining rooms, dining rooms into dens. When you pay attention to the flow of Ch'i through any environment, you will notice its inherent efficiency. Ch'i moves best in the presence of human satisfaction and comfort. Question the way you have set up the rooms in your home and office. You may find spaces you never knew you had.

Exercise:

Stand back and pretend for a moment that no one ever told you how to set up and use your home or workplace. Would you change anything? When an environment is set up to individually serve the people living or working there, the Ch'i is enhanced, and everyone benefits.

Pointing the Way—Corners

Because Western architecture and design are dominated by angular shapes, we end up living in the constant presence of corners. Corners on buildings are considered *offensive* in the true meaning of the word— they shoot strong Ch'i in whatever direction they are pointed. The sharp corners we find on so much of our furniture can be dangerous when made from the typical building materials of glass, wood, metal, or stone. We have all been bruised or cut by furniture that reaches out and bites us with its corners when we're not careful. Their presence breaks one of the cardinal Feng Shui rules: *Always live with things that are safe!*

Furniture, counter, and display corners also become arrows when pointed toward a door. They will actually direct people out the door before they've ever had a chance to come in. Many a store has suffered from a lack of customers because they set up displays that pointed people in the wrong direction—OUT instead of IN. I recently entered a crafts gallery and noticed that all their front displays were set up with their corners facing the door. The feeling of being pushed back out the door was palpable. I asked the manager how business was. She said that most people just stood in the door and looked, but they never came in.

Whether in homes or workplaces, people can be negatively affected by corners. Furniture and structural corners facing the front entrance can make guests or customers feel unwelcome. They can contribute to sending positive influences of all kinds out of the building. When faced toward the interior doors inside a home or office, corners can act like annoying little pointers, jabbing and pushing at people as they pass through a room.

There are several solutions:

- Whenever possible, choose designs and pieces of furniture that do not have sharp corners. Even if the general shape is square or rectangular, softened corners will make them much safer and friendlier.

- When existing furniture and displays already have sharp corners, turn them diagonally so that a flat side is facing the door.

- Soften corners by screening or covering them with things such as fabric and plants.

  Exercise:

  The next time you are in your favorite store, notice how the displays are set up. Are there corners pointed toward you as you enter through the front door? If they are, what is your response to them? See if you feel drawn in or pushed out. Notice the same thing when you're in a store that you don't particularly like. What are the differences you perceive between the way the two stores are designed and arranged?

Reshaping the Box—Corners in Rooms

The corners in a square room have the tendency to pull sharply on the Ch'i that's circulating through the room. Once the Ch'i is pulled into a corner, it tends to stay there and stagnate. The stagnation is exacerbated by the accumulation of objects that really belong elsewhere, such as boxes, papers, and sports equipment. Corners can easily become the stagnant backwaters of a room.

The primary Feng Shui solution for corners in rooms is to soften them by either rounding them out or filling them in. You can literally round out corners using building materials to fill and round out the corners formed by walls, ceilings, doors, and windows. Crown molding, and other types of decorative wood strips can soften the extreme points made by walls, ceilings, and floors joining at right angles. Or, you can soften corners by placing items such as lights, plants, art pieces, baskets, ceramics, and sculpture in front of them. Sometimes, turning furniture at a diagonal to round out a corner is the perfect solution. Corners can also be worked with from above by suspending bells, crystals, wind chimes, mobiles, and any kind of banners and hanging art that appeals to you. Structural corners that jut out into the room can also be unfriendly and are worked with in the same way. Their angular pointed shape requires softening to balance the Ch'i. As explained above, choose a pleasing way to soften the protruding corner.

For most of us, it is a wonderfully unique experience to be inside a structure that has no corners. My husband Brian and I enjoy staying in the Rainbow Hill Inn in Julian, California, built by organic architect James Hubbell. In that entire structure, there isn't one corner. All of the rooms are softly rounded organic shapes sculpted out of adobe. During our visits, we are both filled with a surge of creativity, coupled with a deep calm. We are simultaneously energized and relaxed by the abundance of Ch'i that meanders harmoniously throughout the structure.

Raging Rapids and Rivers—Stairways and Hallways

Other architectural features that are often extreme in their character are stairs and halls. Stairs can become powerful waterfalls of Ch'i, channeling too much of the structure's vital energy down and out into another area. If the stairs point toward the front entrance, the nourishing Ch'i pours right out the door, often taking the health and good fortune of the occupants with it. Rooms located at the top of a flight of stairs are continually pulled on by the force of the nearby descent—just like the area above a natural waterfall—while rooms at the bottom of a stairway are perpetually flooded with the raging Ch'i pouring down from the upper level. Feng Shui seeks to place people out of extreme Ch'i flow, not in the middle of it. Therefore, the treatments for stairs are to bring about balance and peaceful waters.

When you're working with stairways that face doorways, you need to do your best to stop the flow of Ch'i from rolling out the door. This is best done by installing some kind of aesthetic barrier between door and stairs, such as a screen, plants, furniture, or art. When there is no room for this, you can hang a mirror facing the stairs to help lift and circulate the descending Ch'i. You can also hang a round faceted crystal above the bottom step, again to catch and circulate the sliding Ch'i. Be sure not to accentuate the waterfall shape further by hanging art in a descending order down the stairwell. Use your art to help rechannel the Ch'i by hanging it all from the same height, creating one strong horizontal line to keep the Ch'i lifted. Also, choose subject matter that is light and buoyant, which suggests movement back up the stairs, such as birds in flight or an abstract with horizontal or uplifting lines. In some cases, a mirror in the stairwell is appropriate, as long as it's not hung directly across from another mirror.

These Feng Shui adjustments can be used to balance the Ch'i flowing down stairs in any location. Remember to use your Feng Shui eyes, and your Feng Shui ears, too. Let the environment "tell" you the best solution.

Just like stairs, the halls and corridors in your home or office can channel Ch'i too fast for comfort. Long halls speed people up, often causing them to walk very quickly or run, rather than move at a normal pace. It's difficult for most people to stand in a hallway and have a conversation. I find that standing in most hallways is like being thigh-high in a river that's tugging at me forcefully with its strong current. To balance this, hallways need to be broken up into smaller human-friendly parts, or adjusted to be like meandering paths. To break up a wide hall, arrange art, mirrors, lights, furniture, and carpets to suggest a series of rooms or niches and slow down the Ch'i. To suggest a winding path, randomly place points of interest along the corridor using items such as plants, furniture, art, and statuary. This will slow the Ch'i down to a friendly speed and give people a chance to catch their breath.

Placing a mirror at the end of a long corridor is usually inappropriate, because it doubles the length of a feature that's already long enough. However, placing mirrors across from the doors that open onto the hall can be very helpful. Their presence widens the appearance of the hall and adjusts the Ch'i of the people using the hallway doors.

The Line Between Heaven and Earth—Ceilings

Most of us are comfortable in rooms with an 8- to 10-foot ceiling over our heads. If a ceiling is much higher than that, we may begin to feel uncomfortable, small, or disoriented. It can be too "yang," or provide too much space overhead for people's comfort. I have been in many homes where the living room ceiling is over 15 feet tall and, much to the dismay of the people who live there, no one uses the room. Everyone congregates in the kitchen or den area, where the ceiling drops to a comfortable eight feet. People may like the look of a high ceiling as they pass through the room, but they don't want to linger there. They usually don't know exactly why, it's just not where they want to be.

One way to balance the extreme height of the ceiling is to create a "Line Between Heaven and Earth." As a yin influence, this horizontal line defines and grounds the room as it breaks up the vertical height of the ceiling. Draw this line by running one horizontal border around the room that is anywhere from 6 to 10 feet off the floor. This border can follow the natural line begun by the top of doors, windows, art or bookshelves (see Figure 1a on next page). It can be made of crown molding, wallpaper borders, or simply suggested by hanging art at the same height all the way around the room.

Depending on the actual height and size of the ceiling, the "heavenly" space above the line can be a fabulous place to hang a lightweight mobile, banner, flag, or textile art of some kind. An artist in Encinitas, California, Geri Scalone, has designed a "trapeze" on which she hangs

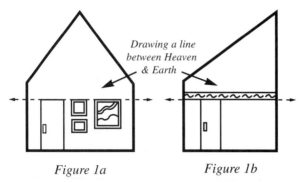

Drawing a line between Heaven & Earth

Figure 1a   *Figure 1b*

fabric collages that can be easily changed by lowering the trapeze, hanging new combinations of materials on it, and hoisting it up again. These art pieces define Heaven in a way that delights the eye and inspires the spirit. The mere suggestion of a comfortable ceiling height, as well as the possible addition of art defining the "heavens" above, is usually all people need to fall in love with a room with a high ceiling and make themselves at home in it.

Rooms that have a high ceiling on one side and drop to a lower level on the other can also feel uncomfortable. You can use the same technique of drawing a line between Heaven and Earth (see Figure 1b). Again, decide on one horizontal line and follow it all the way around the room to visually even out the architecture. The lower wall is a great place to hang a mirror to lift the oppressed Ch'i, while large pieces of furniture are ideally placed on the higher side of the room to help stabilize the Ch'i. Lights and plants also can balance the Ch'i, and can be used in combination with the mirror and the Heaven and Earth line.

Low, flat ceilings present another challenge, compressing the Ch'i with their close proximity. Low ceilings are considered very yin, and therefore need the yang influences of lights, mirrors, plants, and light, bright colors to lift and expand the Ch'i. Include lighting that shines up toward the ceiling, suggesting a vertical, uplifting line. Choose upholstery and art that's vertically striped in some way. The idea is to bring in yang items to balance the yin influence of the low ceiling.

Ch'i Channels—Beams

Exposed beams are a popular structural feature in Western architecture, and are often thought of as adding character to a room. They also add a troublesome sense of heaviness over people's heads. Beams typically hold tremendous weight as part of the structure of the building and can channel strong lines of Ch'i, much as hallways do. The bigger, darker, and lower they are, the more they require Feng Shui balancing.

To bring a beam into balance, there are several things you can do:

- Symbolically break the line of force by placing two pieces of wood (classically, bamboo) at angles (see Figure 2a). This "breaks up" the Ch'i racing along the thoroughfare of the beam, and suggests the beginning of an octagon or a circle, which circulates the Ch'i down and around the room.

- Paint the beam a light color, such as white, beige, or a pastel. This will lift it up and soften its visual presence.

- Balance the beam by hanging textiles, swags, ribbons, banners, mobiles, or other lightweight art objects from them (see Figure 2b). This softens and rounds them out, and adds color and items that represent other elements. When "treating" a beam in this way, use only lightweight items so that no one feels threatened when under them.

- Keep in mind that most beams are made of wood, so the first element for you to consider enhancing is Metal in the form of light colors and rounded shapes.

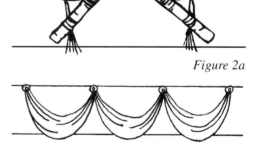

Figure 2a

Figure 2b

Our 20th-Century Companions—Electrical Equipment

Ch'i is activated by electrical equipment. Items such as televisions, computers, stereo equipment, copiers, and microwaves can have a commanding physical and energetic presence that draws attention from the people who live or work near them. Some people say electrical equipment is "insistent," and will stare at their owners or users until they get their attention. In an office environment, this is usually perfect. Everyone's Ch'i is kept activated by the electrical equipment that surrounds them. However, in a home, the equipment can be running the show, keeping everyone activated when they really need to be balancing their busy days with some peace and quiet. Most parents know about the battle that's fought daily with their children about TV and computer use. The equipment is continually "calling" to them to come and play!

One of the best and easiest solutions is to conceal the equipment when not in use. Put it out of sight in cabinets and closets, or cover it with a beautiful cloth. It surprises people how much more peaceful and serene a room feels by simply covering the TV, or putting the stereo in a closed cabinet. This is especially important in a bedroom where a television or a computer screen staring at you can actually interfere with your rest.

Electrical equipment and automobiles have the same tendency to dominate their surroundings. When "out in front," they have a strong, demanding influence on their users. In a home, they are better servants and entertainers when they are placed out of sight between uses. Conversely, in an office, their visibility keeps everything humming and active.

Besides the dominating presence of electrical equipment, there is the very real concern about Electro-Magnetic Radiation (EMR). All electrical equipment emits some quantity of EMR. Usually, it's very little, but equipment such as computers and microwaves can emit enough EMR to be harmful to us. When I tested the EMR of the electrical equipment in our home, I discovered that our fax machine, the TV, and the microwave emitted more EMR than anything else in the house. To be safe, we needed to sit or stand at least six feet away from them when in use. Ideally, all of your electrical equipment should be checked with an EMR tester.

Exercise:

Choose a room in your house that has exposed electrical equipment in it, such as a TV or computer. Sit and look at it for a moment, then conceal it with a pleasing cloth or screen. See if you notice a difference in the Ch'i in the room.

Review

We have discussed many aspects of Feng Shui that pertain to our home and office environments. In brief:

• Our home and work environments are vibrantly alive, completely interconnected with the rest of our lives, and subject to change at any time.

• When our choices in selecting and arranging our environments are focused on comfort and safety, and when we surround ourselves with the things that we love, we enhance the circulation of vital Ch'i. This approach creates our own personal paradise.

• Our choices in selecting and arranging our environments can be made to balance yin and yang qualities and the five elements, which also enhances the circulation of vital Ch'i.

• Our precise choices of the placement of things in our environment can invite people and vital Ch'i in, or it can push people and vital Ch'i away.

Setting Up Your Power Spots—Desks, Beds, and Other Furnishings

The guidelines for working with your furniture are the same as those for your environment. They are as follows:

- Your furniture is essentially alive, interconnected with the rest of your life, and subject to being moved around at any time.

- When your choices in selecting and placing your furniture are focused on creating comfort and safety, and when you surround yourself with pieces that you love, you enhance the circulation of vital Ch'i. This approach will create your own personal paradise.

- Your choices in selecting and arranging your furniture can balance the yin and yang qualities and the five elements, which also enhances the flow of vital Ch'i throughout your environment.

- Your precise choices of the placement of your furniture can invite people and vital Ch'i in, rather than pushing people and vital Ch'i away.

Furniture is important. It surrounds you day and night and supports you in every way. Think of living with absolutely no furniture, and you realize how important it is. You are either using it or looking at it. Each piece of furniture in your home or office has a distinct presence that demands a response. Either you like it, love it, or dislike it. Ideally, you already love every piece of furniture in your home and workplace. If not, begin to plan how you can change your furnishings so that in the near future you will love them all. It could mean that you live without until the perfect piece shows up. Or, make it a priority to find it now, not later. Keeping the Feng Shui principles in mind, you can see how crucial it is to surround yourself with furniture that always pleases, embraces, and supports you.

Creating personal comfort and safety when arranging your furniture also involves finding the "power spots" in each room. This is especially applicable when arranging a piece of furniture that you spend much of your time using, such as a desk or a bed.

You know you are in a power spot in a room when you can see the door leading into the room. If there's more than one door into the room, then you can see all the doors from the power spot, or at least, the primary door. There are very few people who are comfortable sitting or lying down where they can't see the door. It's a deep instinctual response that, when ignored, can jangle people's nervous systems and set them on edge.

Many of us spend most of our waking hours at a desk or work table. It is our power place—the place where we work, have meetings, make phone calls, write, and in general, further our professional lives. Desks and work tables are ideally located in a power place in the room, with a view of the door. If your desk is against a wall, with your back to the door, there are two possible solutions:

- Reposition your desk so that you can see the door.

- Place a mirror on or behind your desk so that you can see the door in the mirror. Mirrors can also be used to reflect the view you may lose when you turn your desk around to see the door.

In one case, a client set up his desk in his home office with his back to the door facing a gorgeous view across a canyon and out to the ocean. He was writing a novel and would become very immersed in his creative musings. Every night at exactly the same time, his wife would come in with their son to say goodnight, and every night the man would nearly jump out of his skin when he realized someone was behind him. He became very irritated with her because she scared him like that every night. Her response was to be very annoyed with *him* for always jumping, and then being so testy with her about it. You'd think he would have gotten used to it! His wife tried calling his name first, clapping, or "yoo-hoo"-ing, and he'd still jump. Even so, he wasn't willing to turn his desk around because he loved and was inspired by the awesome view.

Our solution was to place a standing mirror, often called a shaving mirror, on his desk, and he never jumped again. His eye would catch the first movements of his wife and son coming in the door, and he was fine from then on.

In a business setting, everyone's life, from the president of the company to the receptionist in the lobby, pivots around their desks. Since many offices suffer from a long list of Ch'i-depleting conditions including crowded work areas, low ceilings, and fluorescent lighting, it's even more crucial for workers to balance and enliven the Ch'i on and around their desks.

First and foremost, desks need to have a view of the door, either directly, or via a mirror. This is one of the easiest and most powerful enhancements you can make. Use plants, screens, or false fronts when computer and other wires need to be camouflaged. Enjoy personalizing your desk area with items that you love and that nourish your Ch'i throughout the day. Take a look at the chapter on Basic Feng Shui Tools on page 155, as well as Mapping the Bagua of Your Furniture (page 72). Enjoy building an energizing, revitalizing circle of Ch'i, using your desk as the foundation.

Exercise:

When you want to reposition your desk and have two or more places in the room from which you can see the door, put your desk chair in each of those spots first. Position the chair exactly as it would be if your desk was there, sit quietly for a few minutes, and get a sense of what it would feel like to spend time there. In most cases, there will be one spot that immediately feels right—this is your power spot.

A bed is another piece of furniture that, when well placed, assures a good night's sleep and a feeling of safety and comfort. This is important because we spend a third of our lives in bed, and it's the time when we are most vulnerable.

Beds are trickier than desks for two reasons. First, mirrors don't really belong in bedrooms. They activate the Ch'i in a room meant for rest and relaxation, and they reflect movement that can frighten a half-asleep person. Believe it or not, mirrored closet doors in bedrooms are more of a Feng Shui problem than a benefit. The rule of thumb is to have one mirror or less in the bedroom, hung as far away from the bed as possible. A bedroom should feel like a safe, restful nest, not an elaborate dressing room.

I was recently called to a home where the teenage son hadn't had a decent night's sleep since the family had moved in a month earlier. He insisted on keeping a light on throughout the night because the room gave him "the creeps." His bedroom included an entire wall of mirrored closet doors, large enough to make it impossible to locate the bed away from them. We discussed the options of either replacing the mirrored doors with regular doors, or curtaining them so that they could be opened during the day and closed at night. The boy's mom decided she'd temporarily curtain them that night by simply pinning up a couple of sheets. Her son immediately felt better in the room and has been sleeping soundly throughout the night without a light on ever since.

The second reason that bed placement is tricky is that the power of the bed lies in how rested and rejuvenated a person feels as a result of sleeping in it. It needs to feel cloistered and secluded, while still having a view of the door. Therefore, a bed placed directly in the path of a door isn't ideal, even though a person can see the door from it. Ideal placement is off to one side of the door, out of the direct line of Ch'i, but where the door can still be seen.

Other furniture such as easy chairs, sofas, and dining room tables and chairs can be situated to provide as much of a view of the door as possible. When furniture needs to be faced away from the door, consider hanging a mirror so that the door can be seen in its reflection. Remember, people are most comfortable when they feel in control of their environment and can see what's going on in a room.

Exercise:

Next time you have guests over, invite them to sit anywhere they'd like, and notice where they sit. Usually, the seating that faces the door will be taken first.

▼▼▼ ▼▼▼

In choosing your dwelling,
  know how to keep to the
  ground.
In cultivating your mind,
  know how to dive in the hidden
  depths.
In dealing with others,
  know how to be gentle and kind.
In speaking,
  know how to keep your word.
In governing,
  know how to maintain order.
In transacting business,
  know how to be efficient.
In making a move,
  know how to choose the right
  moment.

—Lao Tzu

THE I CHING AND
FENG SHUI'S BAGUA MAP

The Bagua Map (see next page) originates from the I Ching, or Book of Changes, an ancient Chinese book of divination. The word *Bagua* describes the eight basic building blocks of the I Ching, called *trigrams*. Each trigram is associated with specific "treasures" in life, such as health, wealth, and love. In the practice of Feng Shui, the Bagua is used to map out homes and office buildings and locate the areas that correspond to the various treasures, giving every part of the building significance and meaning. According to Feng Shui, the good fortune of the inhabitants is significantly strengthened when the Bagua of their home or workplace has been properly mapped out and enhanced.

My experience in working with the Bagua Map is that it is one of the most powerful ways to create positive changes and results in your life. Homes, office buildings, condominium complexes, gardens, rooms, and even furniture can be mapped out using this potent tool. I have seen it produce results that appear amazing and magical.

The successful results produced by the Bagua occur from combin-

The Bagua Map

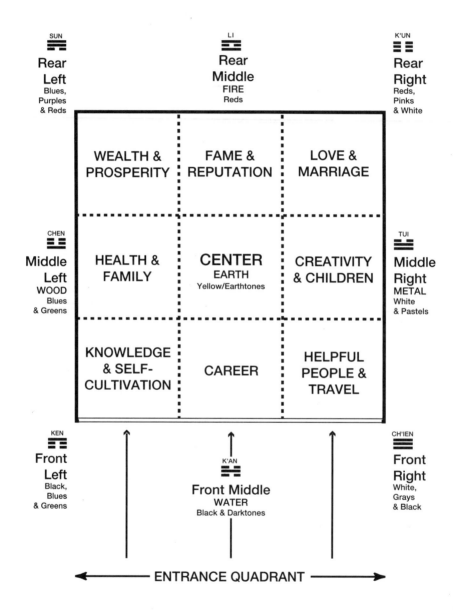

SUN
Rear
Left
Blues,
Purples
& Reds

LI
Rear
Middle
FIRE
Reds

K'UN
Rear
Right
Reds,
Pinks
& White

WEALTH & PROSPERITY	FAME & REPUTATION	LOVE & MARRIAGE
HEALTH & FAMILY	CENTER EARTH Yellow/Earthtones	CREATIVITY & CHILDREN
KNOWLEDGE & SELF-CULTIVATION	CAREER	HELPFUL PEOPLE & TRAVEL

CHEN
Middle
Left
WOOD
Blues
& Greens

TUI
Middle
Right
METAL
White
& Pastels

KEN
Front
Left
Black,
Blues
& Greens

K'AN
Front Middle
WATER
Black & Darktones

CH'IEN
Front
Right
White,
Grays
& Black

← ENTRANCE QUADRANT →

ing two forces. The first is the timeless wisdom that the I Ching provides. The second is the user's serious intention to produce a positive change in life. Over the last six years, I've observed repeatedly that when a person seeking positive change in his or her life, places objects that are personally meaningful in areas correlated with the Bagua Map, the Ch'i is aligned and quickened to produce the desired result. *And quickly!* Just like many types of treatments for our bodies, when the right Bagua "remedy" has been applied, a positive change occurs that directly relates to the person's desires and goals in less than 30 days. If no change occurs in that time, the person needs to take another look through their Feng Shui eyes at the Bagua Map and at their true intentions, and adjusts the Bagua enhancements they've chosen for the specific area they're working with. When taken seriously, just like a meditation or a treatment, positive results are inevitable.

Locating Your Treasures—How to Use the Bagua Map

Imagine a birds-eye view of the building you're mapping, and determine its overall shape. It may be a square, a rectangle, or a shape like a T, S, U, or L. Garages and additions of any kind under the same roof are included when defining the shape. There are some buildings that have such complex shapes that it is challenging to figure out exactly how to apply the Bagua Map. If this is the case with you, there are two things you can do. You can apply the Bagua Map to the rooms inside the building and work with it that way. Or, you can contact, me and we can figure it out together. (Information on how to reach me is at the back of this book.)

Once you've determined the overall shape, stand facing the front entrance to the building as if you are about to step inside. As the primary Mouth of Ch'i, your front entrance is your vantage point for determining the orientation of the Bagua Map for the whole building. Even when you usually come and go through a garage or back door, your official front entrance is used to determine the Bagua. Whatever the shape of your building is, fit it completely inside the Bagua Map so that the entire structure is within the nine sections of the Map. Even if

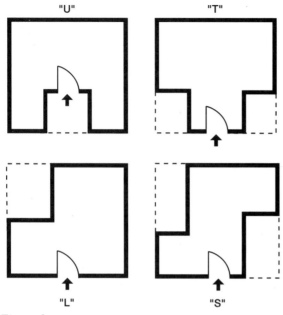

Figure 3

your front entrance is recessed, it is still facing the same direction as the front of the Bagua Map. If the building is a shape such as an L, T, S, or U, there will be Bagua areas on the Map that will be outside the structure of the building (see Figure 3). If the building is square (as in the illustrated Bagua Map), rectangular, or circular, it is considered a whole shape, and the Bagua Map is stretched to accommodate them. Small structural protrusions such as bay windows or fireplaces can act as enhancements of the Bagua area they are located in. Indentations in the structure usually need to be worked with like a missing area.

As the Bagua Map shows, when your front entrance is on the left side of the front of the building, it is located in your Knowledge and Self-Cultivation area. If the front door is in the center of the front of the building, it's in your Career area, and if it's on the right side, you are entering through the Helpful People and Travel area.

Once you've determined which Bagua area your front door is in, the rest of the areas can be easily located. For instance, to locate your Wealth and Prosperity area, use the front entrance as your vantage point and determine the rear left section of the building. If the structure has more than one story, the Wealth and Prosperity area will carry through and be in the same place on each floor. For example, if your dining room is located in the rear left section of your home, with a bedroom directly above it, that bedroom would also be in the Wealth and Prosperity area of the house.

Now, determine the rear right section of the building. This is the area associated with Love and Marriage. As you follow the Bagua Map around, you can see that between your Wealth area and your Love area is your Fame and Reputation section in the middle rear of the building. Locate your Health and Family section on the middle left side between the Wealth and Prosperity and Knowledge and Self-Cultivation areas. Your Creativity and Children section is located on the middle right side between your Love and Marriage and Helpful People and Travel areas. Notice as you follow the Map around if any areas are actually outside the building's structure.

Mapping the Bagua of a Room

To chart the Bagua of each room, stand at the door and look into the room. If there is more than one door into the room, stand at the one most frequently used. This is your vantage point for determining the Bagua orientation of the room, just as a front entrance determines the Bagua orientation of a building. A door on the left side of a room is in the Knowledge and Self-Cultivation area, while a door in the middle of a room is in the Career section. An entrance on the right side of a room is in the Helpful People and Travel area. Many times, the Bagua areas of each room will *not* coincide with the Bagua areas of the building, nor do they need to. You will find that each room has its own Bagua areas to work with and enhance. Therefore, by the time you've figured out the Bagua for a building, as well as for the rooms inside, you will have plenty of Bagua areas to work with! Do not feel that you have to enhance every Bagua area in every room. *Work first with the areas that are associated with the areas in your life you'd like to enhance.*

In general, the Bagua of any building is considered more important than the Bagua of each room because it holds more structural Ch'i. Nevertheless, when Bagua areas have been enhanced in the rooms of a building, the Ch'i flows with a dynamic, harmonious flair, uplifting the people who live or work there.

Matching Room Functions to the Bagua Map

As you will probably discover, matching the function of your rooms to the Bagua Map of the building is usually impossible. In other words, to have your master bedroom in the Love and Marriage area, your office in the Career or Wealth area, your kitchen in the Health and Family area, and your studio in the Creativity area is not how most houses are set up. It would be nice, but it's not vitally important. What really is important is to make sure all your areas are organized, and that the ones you are working with are enhanced to the best of your ability. For instance, if your master bedroom is located in the Bagua area of your house that is associated with Wealth and Prosperity, the most important thing to do is to put a symbol of wealth there, such as a beautiful crystal vase or a rich-looking comforter across the bed. What if a Love and Marriage area is located in the bathroom? This is a great location for objects that represent love, sensuality, and intimacy, such as erotic art, scented candles, and velvety towels. Every room, no matter what its primary function is, can incorporate a Bagua symbol that has personal meaning and substance.

Missing Bagua Areas

If any Bagua area is outside the structure of the building, it is considered missing, and you will want to include it either literally or symbolically into the overall structure. When literally working with a missing area of a building, you can complete its shape by filling in the missing area with a structure such as a covered porch or room addition (see Figure 4). Decks, patios, and arbors can also serve the purpose when they have enough structural substance to be considered part of the building. You can strengthen these features even further by appointing them with colors and objects that relate to the Bagua areas they're completing. For instance, if there is a deck with an arbor in the Love and Marriage area of a home, the occupants could add white, pink, and red flowers; garden art depicting lovers; and/or white outdoor furniture.

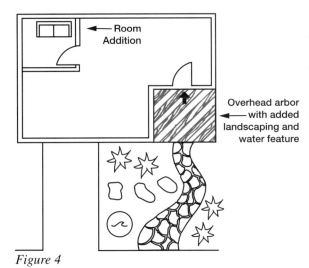

Figure 4

You can also complete a missing area by using symbolic additions, or those that do not physically change the shape of the house, but define the missing area outdoors. When planning symbolic additions, first find the place where the corner of the building would be if it were squared off (see Figure 5). That area is then filled in with sizable and aesthetically pleasing combinations of things such as:

- Fencing
- An outdoor lamppost
- A flagpole
- Landscaping that includes large boulders and substantial plants and/or trees
- Water features, such as fountains or waterfalls
- Sculpture

If you happen to live or work in a building where a Bagua area is "missing," and you cannot do anything to enhance the structure from the outside, there are ways you can symbolically work with the structure

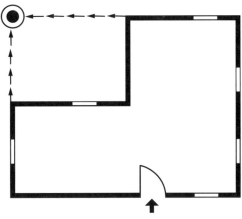

Figure 5

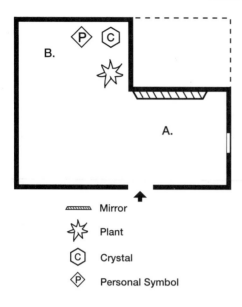

B.

A.

⟨ᗰᗰᗰᗰ⟩ Mirror

✧ Plant

Ⓒ Crystal

Ⓟ Personal Symbol

Figure 6 A & B

from the inside. Mirroring the indented wall or walls closest to the missing Bagua area can make the indentation seem to disappear, and enhance the circulation of Ch'i (see section A of Figure 6). If there are windows in that area, hang a round faceted crystal, and place a beautiful plant there to enliven and circulate the Ch'i (see section B). Placing your own personal Bagua enhancements there will further strengthen the Ch'i. Missing areas make it even more important to enliven the corresponding Bagua areas in other rooms. For instance, if your Wealth area is outside the structure of your condominium, you would want to make sure to enhance the Wealth areas in every room to lift and strengthen the Wealth Ch'i of your home.

The Bagua Map and Living with What You Love

Once you have familiarized yourself with the Bagua Map, take a look around you. Do you see things that you love and cherish? Are they things that anchor your dreams and remind you of your blessings and goals in life? Take a visual inventory of what surrounds you. As you look around, ask, "What do I love?" What has wonderful memories attached to it? What doesn't? What makes me feel rich and powerful, loved and joyful? What has "poor and powerless" written all over it? What holds good memories, and what doesn't?

The idea is to identify and observe where the Ch'i-depleters, the things that drain your energy, and the Ch'i-builders, the things the strengthen your energy, are located in your environment. Then compare their location with the Bagua areas you want to work with. Very often, there is an object that depletes the Ch'i right in the middle of a Bagua area you'd actually like to enhance. One woman complained that her romantic relationships were not working, and in her Love and Marriage area stood a large clock that didn't work. Another woman reported feeling creatively blocked. She discovered that her Creativity and Children area was in her garage, where things she didn't need in the house had been thrown into a chaotic pile.

Take a look at where your Ch'i-builders are in relation to the Bagua Map. These objects are often located in areas associated with aspects of life that are going quite well. A happily married couple discovered that they had hung their favorite photographs of themselves in their Love and Marriage area. A man who enjoyed professional success found that he'd located his large fish aquarium in his Career area.

Sorting your belongings for what you love, and therefore, for what builds and enhances Ch'i, can be challenging. It involves looking through your Feng Shui eyes at possessions you may have never questioned before. Keep asking yourself, "Do I really love this, and do I really need this?" As you do so, it's helpful to remember that the Ch'i in everything is "talking" to you—impacting you—all the time. Make sure you're surrounding yourself with compliments and blessings, not whines and lectures. Your material possessions can be a blessing if they're things that nourish you, or a curse if they're things that don't. For many people, possessions stack up and become "toxic" and Ch'i-depleting. Keep the Ch'i strong and lively in your environment by removing the possessions you don't love and living with the possessions you do.

The Sea of Ch'i that flows through your environments can be mapped out and sculpted into perfect harmony by your own hands. The Bagua Map is your guide. Get ready. It's my experience that your call for positive change is always answered.

Environmental Affirmations—Personalizing Your Bagua Enhancements

When enhancing the Bagua areas of your home and workplace with symbols and items that have positive personal meaning to you, they become powerful "Environmental Affirmations," magnifying and intensifying the positive Ch'i in your life. Your environmental affirmations physically and energetically build the Ch'i, setting into motion a direct call for the changes you are choosing to focus on—whether it's increasing wealth, nourishing love, producing work, supporting creativity, or improving your health. The call is strengthened every time you see or think about your Bagua enhancements, affirming time and again that you are ready for the positive changes you are seeking.

You can begin working with the Bagua Map by using one or more of the Basic Feng Shui Tools listed in Chapter 8 (page 155). For many people, these enhancements already have or quickly take on personal meaning, and therefore work well to enhance their Bagua areas. But before you begin buying crystals or wind chimes, take a look at the Personalized Enhancements listed at the end of each Bagua Success Story. Then, look around your home and see if you already have the perfect enhancements for the Bagua areas you want to work with. Often, people have "all the right things in all the wrong places."

When you don't find something to enhance a Bagua area that speaks to you, consider creating it yourself. You can draw, sculpt, build, assemble, write, or paint something that has your own personal Ch'i in it. Have fun being innovative when enhancing your Bagua areas. Drawing from the depth of your creative resources can be deeply satisfying and empowering. Keep in mind that the more personal—the more near and dear to your heart—your Bagua enhancement is, the more imbued it is with your personal Ch'i, and therefore the more powerful it is.

Whether you want to enhance the Wealth and Prosperity Bagua of your office, the Creativity area of your studio, or the Love area of your home, I recommend that you place something there immediately. Don't wait for the right time to begin your Bagua enhancements. Even if it's just a meaningful picture taped to the wall, begin now!

Every Place Counts: Closets, Basements, Attics, Garages

Because the Bagua areas are located throughout the entire structure you're working with, one or more Bagua areas will inevitably be in your garage, basement, closets, and bathroom. Therefore, these areas are as important as any other room in your home or office. "There is no place to hide" is the operating principle here. You may be the only one who sees a chaotic closet or a disorganized garage, but YOU are the one who's being constantly affected by the Ch'i there.

Think of opening a closet door and seeing everything clearly organized inside. Now think of opening the same closet door and seeing the contents in complete chaos. It's likely that you will have two very different responses to these two scenarios. Add to that the knowledge that the closet is in one of your Bagua areas, and is affecting the quality of the Ch'i habitually surrounding you. If chaos resides anywhere in your home or office, it's time to get organized—completely organized. It's time to take stock of the material possessions that live with you and the Ch'i they emanate.

Experience has taught me how challenging this task can be. We tend to store things we're not using for some reason. Asking why is crucial. Look in the most chaotic storage area in your home and ask two questions: "Do I really need this?" and "Do I really love this?" The answer should be yes to at least one of the questions, and preferably to both. If you're storing a possession because it's useful during a particular season or time, then your job is to give it a neat, clearly defined place to be. If you're storing a possession because you have no clue what to do with it, don't like it, it's worn out, it's broken, or it doesn't fit, then consider passing it on, throwing it away, selling it, or fixing it. Remember, this exercise in dealing with your "stuff" is all about clearing out the draining, stagnant, unfriendly Ch'i from your home or workplace. It applies to ALL storage spaces, from a three-car garage to a jewelry box.

As you separate out the possessions that you truly need and love, you are essentially exhaling old, debilitating Ch'i and inhaling fresh, vital Ch'i. You activate a healthful circle of giving and receiving, creating a void that is then filled up with something that has the fresh lively Ch'i that supports and nourishes you. Your environment, a direct extension of you, then breathes like a healthy body—free of toxins and excess weight. Being conscious of your possessions is one of the quickest ways to create a personal paradise!

Getting Carried Away—Bathrooms

The expressions: "I might as well have flushed my (money, time, etc.) down the toilet," and "The whole (project, marriage, etc.) went down the drain," are taken very seriously when practicing Feng Shui and enhancing the Bagua. Toilets, and the bathrooms they are located in, can be a threat to the nourishing Ch'i that flows through buildings. Bathrooms have one function: the removal of human waste via the sink, bathtub, shower, and toilet. And, when bathroom drains are left open, the Ch'i in the surrounding area tends to be literally drawn down them. The toilet is especially problematic because of the size of the opening. Keeping the lid down on the toilet seat when it is not in use is mandatory when you want to keep the vital Ch'i flowing throughout your home and office. Many people close all the bathroom drains when not in use.

Ideally, bathrooms are pleasant areas to spend time in, and they can be appointed with the objects and colors that you love, and which relate to the Bagua area they are located in.

Mapping the Bagua of Your Furniture

The Bagua Map may be superimposed on any structure, from huge buildings to a tiny table. Arranging surfaces such as desks, bureaus, and tables according to the Bagua can set the stage for daily success and happiness. As always, the Bagua works best when you have a strong, positive link to the objects you use for enhancements. Since every object is constantly "talking to you," use this concept to your advantage, putting all the right things in all the right places. Surfaces become creative works of artful placement, holding objects that are personally powerful and attractive, balancing and enhancing the Ch'i flowing from and around them. To get started, you may want to take a look at Chapter 8 (Basic Feng Shui Tools), the Personalized Enhancements located at the end of each Bagua Success Story, and the following suggestions. Remember to choose things to which you feel drawn.

Let's use the heart of your workplace—the desk—as an example. Take the Bagua Map and lay it down on your desk. Your "entrance" is where you sit, probably in the middle of the front, in the Career area. From your seat, look to the far left corner of the desk to find your Wealth area. From there, you can follow the Map around your desk to determine the rest of your Bagua areas.

In your Wealth area, you can place things that have a general association with wealth and prosperity, such as a calculator, adding machine, or change bowl. You probably also have things that are directly associated to your wealth and abundance, such as the first dollar bill you earned in your business, pictures or samples of products you sell, or a photo of your biggest client. Other objects that are often used are symbolic, such as a small water feature, a beautiful vase of flowers, a red cloth, or crystal paperweight.

In the back center of your desk is the Fame and Reputation area, a perfect place to display diplomas, awards, or certificates. Other things can symbolize your fame and reputation, such as a bright lamp, a blooming plant, or a framed quotation.

The Love area is in the back right corner of your desk. This is a wonderful spot to show off a photograph of your lover or spouse. Anything that reminds you of love and romance can be placed there, such as a memento from a special weekend, romantic art, or two flowers in a white, pink, or red vase.

Next is the Children and Creativity area, found midway down the right side of your desk. This is a great place to display photos of your children. If you want to have children, this is the perfect place to put a picture of a baby or youngster, including baby animals and budding flowers. Other choices are symbols of creativity, such as vessels of brightly colored pencils, crayons, or marker pens. A framed piece of child's art is great, as well as pictures of people creating artistic works, such as potters, painters, and sculptors.

The Helpful People and Travel area, directly to your right, is a perfect place for the telephone. Other choices for enhancing this area are any cherished mementos from a trip, photographs of mentors, or any spiritual or religious images, calendars, or sayings you find empowering.

Typically, you are sitting in the Career area with an active work space in front of you. This is the area that is often in chaos as you work on your various projects, duties, and so on. What's important here is to keep your Career area cycling through chaos back into order again. Give yourself the gift of keeping this cycle as current as possible. In other words, complete, put away, and begin again on a daily or regular basis so that your work Ch'i doesn't stagnate under piles of papers or supplies.

The Knowledge and Self-Cultivation area is a great spot for current work, reference materials, and books. Whether it's skiing, meditating, or night school, things that represent your newly acquired knowledge also belong here.

The area representing your Health and Family is on the left side of the desk between the Wealth and Knowledge areas. Photos and cards from family and friends are wonderful here, along with flowers and plants, or images calling to mind ideal health and fitness.

In some offices, people do not have the luxury of freely enhancing their desks. There may be a strict code that defines what can and cannot be visible. Even when this is true, the Bagua can be subtly enhanced. For instance, my friend Sean worked in a large and very formal law office where no personal possessions were allowed on the desks. To enhance this area, he placed his IN and OUT files in his Knowledge area, a healthy potted plant in the Health and Family area, his calculator in his Wealth area, a company paperweight in the Fame and Reputation area, his desk lamp in his Love area, his pens and pencils in the Creativity area, and his telephone in the Helpful People area. He chose a black blotter to be in front of him in his Career area, along with his computer. Under each of these objects, he put a short length of ribbon in the color(s) associated with each Bagua area. Even though the ribbons couldn't be seen, Sean knew that they were there and felt that the colors further enhanced the auspicious Ch'i flowing around his desk.

You can create special Bagua arrangements on any surface, including bureaus and tabletops. Your whole environment can be punctuated with objects that have special meaning—placed according to the Bagua Map—enhancing and enlivening the vital Ch'i all around you.

Can success change a person so
completely between one dawn and
another? Can it make one feel taller,
more alive, handsomer, uncommonly
gifted and indomitably secure with
the certainty that this is the way life
will always be? It can and it does!

—*Moss Hart*

7

BAGUA
SUCCESS STORIES

The stories on the following pages illustrate some of the successes my clients have enjoyed when working with the Bagua Map in their own environments. They are included to demonstrate how to work with both the Bagua and Feng Shui principles in general. I have chosen stories that illustrate how quickly, and sometimes even dramatically, a positive change can occur when working with the powerful combination of intention and placement. And, as the stories describe, the changes can be quite surprising. As I stated previously, a positive change in your life that correlates with the Bagua area you are working with should manifest in less than 30 days. If it doesn't, don't give up! Look again at what you've placed in the area, and at your intention, and decide what you can change or reinforce that would make it even better. Remember, you are the master arranger and Ch'i builder of every alive, interconnected, and dynamic thing that surrounds you. Focus on your intention, let the environment be your constant affirmation, and watch what happens.

The Bagua Map
HEALTH AND FAMILY

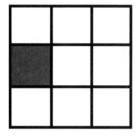

The Health and Family area is located in the middle left side of the structure you are working with, between Knowledge and Self-Cultivation, and Wealth and Prosperity. (See the Bagua Map on page 62).

The I Ching's Wisdom on Health and Family

Health and Family are both associated with the I Ching trigram, *Chen*, translated as the "Shocking Influence of Thunder." This teaching addresses the importance of cultivating strong physical health, and loving family relations to act as supportive foundations through the periodic shocks and unforeseen "storms" of life. "Family" is defined as both our close friends and our blood relatives. Good health and positive family relations assure as much as possible that we will swim and not sink in bad times. These solid foundations of health and family also provide the springboard for expansion, growth, and happiness in life. The healthier we are, the more options we have to exercise, play sports, travel, work, and physically enjoy life. Likewise, the healthier our relationships are with our friends and family, the more we prosper from the opportunities and emotional support they provide. According to the I Ching, auspicious opportunities are best assured, and inauspicious times are best survived, when good physical health and emotional relations are solidly in place.

Enhance your Health and Family areas when:

- your health needs a boost;
- you are planning, or recovering from, surgery;
- you are competing in sports;
- you would like your social life and your "family of choice" to grow or improve in some way; or
- you would like your relationship with relatives to improve.

Stories About Health and Family Bagua in Action

MUDROOMS AND MANSIONS

Joan called me because she was deeply concerned about her husband Charles' physical condition. Since they had moved into their new home a year before, his health had been going steadily downhill. He had recently been forced to give up his work and now spent most of his time in bed. When I asked Joan about her own health, she admitted that she was feeling lethargic and lacked the energy she remembered having had before their move. We made an appointment for the next day.

When I arrived, I was struck by how gracious and beautifully appointed their home was. However, my primary concern was to look at the Health and Family area of the house. As it turned out, it was in a dark little "mudroom," closed off from the rest of the house and devoid of any decoration except the cat's litter box. It was remarkably different from the rest of the house, as was the smell! As serious as her complaint was, Joan just couldn't help but laugh when she realized the condition of the Health and Family area of her home.

Treatments and Results:

We moved the litter box to the downstairs powder room, and brought a lamp and a wooden table into the mudroom.

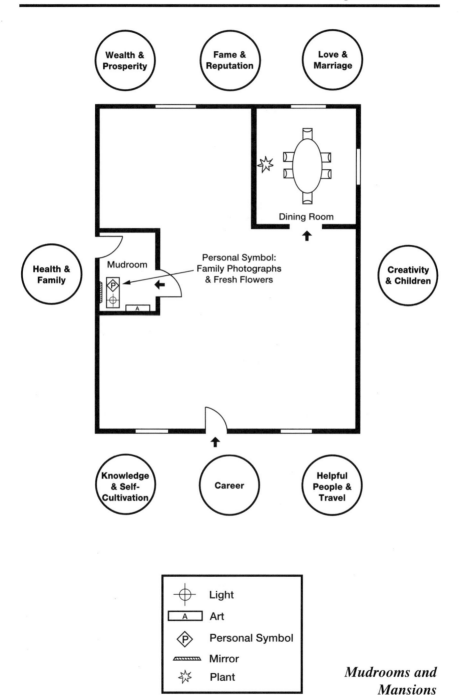

Wealth & Prosperity

Fame & Reputation

Love & Marriage

Health & Family

Mudroom

Personal Symbol:
Family Photographs
& Fresh Flowers

Dining Room

Creativity & Children

Knowledge & Self-Cultivation

Career

Helpful People & Travel

Light
Art
Personal Symbol
Mirror
Plant

Mudrooms and Mansions

We placed fresh flowers on the table to symbolize vibrant health, as well as a favorite family photograph to represent family love. I suggested that Joan leave the door open and the lamp on all the time as a constant reminder of her and her husband's rejuvenating health until they experienced some improvement. To stimulate the Ch'i to flow freely in and out of the area, I asked Joan to hang a mirror framed in wood over the table and to keep the door to the room open. To further enhance the Ch'i and enliven the space, I suggested that she and Charles choose art for the room that they both associated with optimum health, and which included the colors of all five elements. We talked about the much larger project of taking out the wall separating the mudroom from the family room to integrate it with the rest of the house.

We then walked around the rest of the house to look at the Health and Family area in each room and discuss enhancements. Joan decided she would move the largest and most beautiful plant in the house into the Health area in the dining room. As we walked from room to room, she commented that she had all the right things in all the wrong places. She could hardly wait to get started moving things around!

Charles' health took an immediate turn for the better. I believe we "removed the splinter," and he was no longer being affected by the dark and stagnant Ch'i in the Health area of his home. Nourished by all the personal things related to Health and Family that he and Joan placed around their home in "just the right places," Charles fully recovered his health over the next few months. And, Joan's lethargy quickly vanished as she plunged into something she loves to do—remodeling!

▼▼▼

BATHROOM IN THE FAST TRACK

In 45 years, Carol had suffered only three sprains. Her wrist, her finger, and her foot had been sprained as a result of three separate falls in just the last eight months. She knew enough about Feng Shui to assume that there could be a correlation between her sudden clumsiness and the fact that she had moved into her present house nine months ago. She asked me to pay her a visit.

Looking through my Feng Shui eyes, I saw that Carol lived in an almost perfect house. It was square, with all the Bagua areas structurally intact. The garage was a separate building in the back, making the front door the most prominent entrance into the house. The location was a classic armchair configuration, with the house sitting above the street, embraced by a natural hill in back, and enclosed on both sides by mature hedges. Everything was so perfect outside that I was very curious to see Carol's Health and Family area inside the house. It turned out to be the only big glitch in her home's otherwise harmonious Ch'i flow. The one bathroom in the house was located there. And, it was a "Jack and Jill" bath, built between two bedrooms. Each of the two bedrooms opened to the bathroom, and the doors were directly across from each other.

"This configuration tends to speed up the Ch'i, as it passes through the bathroom, especially when the doors are kept open," I explained to Carol. "Living with the rushing Ch'i can cause you to move too quickly. What was happening when you fell?"

Carol smiled and shook her head as she remembered her falls. "This is amazing. In all three cases, I was rushing to do something, and I wasn't being careful. Then I was brought to a screaming halt by falling. So now what? I can't move the bathroom!"

Treatments and Results:

We discussed all the adjustments that Carol could make in the bathroom to balance the Ch'i—like keeping the bathroom doors closed as much as possible. This would create three distinct areas in which the Ch'i could flow, one in each

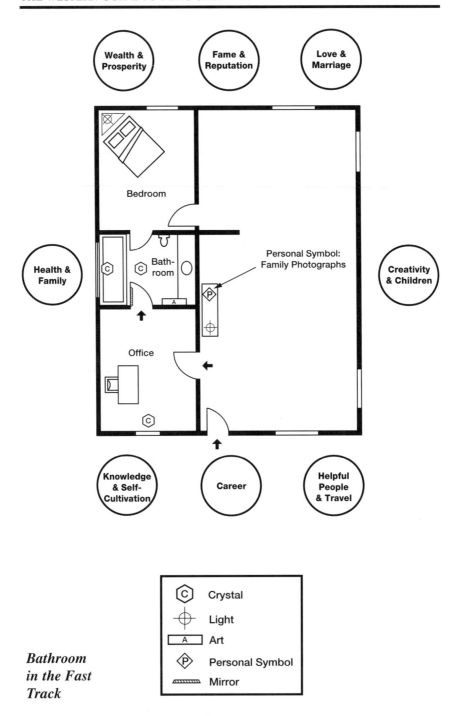

*Bathroom
in the Fast
Track*

bedroom, and one in the bathroom, rather than one "raging river" that plummeted through when the doors were open.

Second, Carol needed to keep the bathroom drains closed when not in use, especially the toilet. This would keep the Ch'i lifted, and give it a chance to circulate through and nourish the area. To draw more vital Ch'i into the bathroom and assure its circulation, I suggested that she hang two round faceted crystals, one in the window to draw the Ch'i in from outdoors, and one in the middle of the room to balance the Ch'i between the two doors. The crystals would also help balance the Ch'i when the bathroom doors were left open.

I looked at the one piece of framed art in the bathroom. I asked Carol how she felt about it.

"Well, it was left over from doing the rest of the house, so I hung it in here. It's okay, I guess."

"Given the crucial Bagua area this bathroom is located in, I'd suggest that you put something you think is great in here, something that really symbolizes good health to you."

Carol was all for changing the art, and we left the bathroom with the existing art under her arm.

Next, I recommended that she hang a wardrobe mirror on the outside of the bathroom door that led into the front bedroom. "Since you're using this room as an office," I said, "the mirror will further boost your productive Ch'i and enhance your creativity. However, I would not suggest a mirror on the door that leads to your bedroom in the back. Seeing movement can be very startling when you're half asleep and need to get up during the night. And along with the mirror in your office, consider hanging a faceted crystal in the front window to further enhance your Health and Family Ch'i."

We walked through the rest of the compact house, looking at the Health and Family areas in each room. Carol's living room included a beautiful collection of lamps. On a credenza in the Health area of the room was the smallest of her collection.

"Which is your favorite lamp?" I asked.

"This one," Carol said, pointing to the Knowledge area

of the room, where a lamp stood made from a beautiful bronze sculpture of a woman holding flowers.

"I'd like to suggest that you move her into your Health area, and keep her lit throughout the day for a while," I said. "She can be your environmental affirmation for perfect health and loving family and friends."

Carol agreed and immediately moved her "healing lady" to her new home on the credenza. As we talked, she also moved her display of family photos out of the Career area of the living room to the credenza, creating a beautiful Health and Family still-life of lamp and photos.

"My parents are still upset that I moved to California," she said. "My patience has been tried by their attitude, and I want us to get along again."

Over the next month, Carol hung her crystals and her mirror, and made a beautiful collage for the bathroom of images that made her think of perfect health. I talked to her recently, about four months after our meeting.

"All I can say is I've been healthy, and I haven't fallen since you were here," she said. "I seem to be calmer in general, even when my parents were visiting me last month."

"How did it go?" I asked.

"Better than I expected—they stayed here at the house, and we had a great time. So, get this—my father never got used to having to put all the toilet seats down, and neither one of them could remember to close the bathroom doors. But, for the sake of good family relations, I stopped trying to train them in Feng Shui bathroom protocol, and would just close the lids and doors myself. Now that they're back home again, Mom says Dad is closing the toilet lids, and she's hung a mirror on the outside of the door. My parents are actually practicing good Feng Shui—I love it!"

Personalized Enhancements for Health and Family

You can use one or a combination of the following items to personally enhance the Health and Family area:

- Healthy plants of all kinds
- Fresh cut flowers in all colors
- Posters, paintings, collages, photos; and figures of ideal body images, family and friends, plants and flowers, gardens and landscapes
- Items in the colors of blue and green
- All things made from wood, including furniture and decorations
- All floral prints, such as floral linens, upholstery, and wallpaper
- Quotes, affirmations, and sayings pertaining to the ideal Health and Family
- Other things that have a personal association to Health and Family, such as mementos, athletic awards, heirlooms, etc.

Affirmations for Health and Family

Choose the affirmations you like from the list below, write them down, and display them in the Health and Family area of your home, office, room, or desk. Or, use these affirmations as a guide in writing your own personal affirmations.

I am a vibrantly healthy person.

My health is excellent in every way.

I enjoy wonderful relationships with my family.

I enjoy harmonious relationships with my friends.

I am blessed with vibrant health and loving relationships.

▼▼▼

The Bagua Map
WEALTH AND PROSPERITY

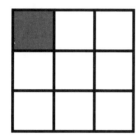

Your Wealth and Prosperity area is located at the rear left section of the structure you are working with. (See the Bagua Map, page 62.)

The I Ching's Wisdom on Wealth and Prosperity

Wealth and Prosperity are associated with the I Ching trigram, *Sun*, translated as the "Persistent Influence of Wind." This teaching is focused on the honest, safe, and gradual accumulation of wealth as an ideal path. When we take our time "shaping" our wealth through slow and steady persistence, adopting the yin qualities of patience, trust, and self-control, we build a solid financial foundation. In this way, much like the wind slowly shaping a rock or tree, we are the most likely to enjoy each day while financially securing our future. High-risk ventures are typically very yang in their nature, and like high winds, they can be unpredictable. They hold the potential of bringing fabulous gains or devastating losses. According to the I Ching, the steady and gradual accumulation of wealth is the best path for securing present and future happiness.

Happiness comes to us in many forms. There is great value in having close friends and family, good health, and fulfilling creative expression in the world. The ideal way to build and maintain the things that are valuable to us is likened to the gentle, steady influence of a warm breeze. When we caress the people, places, and things that bring the experience of abundance and prosperity into our lives, we are living according to this I Ching teaching.

▼▼▼

Enhance your Wealth and Prosperity areas when:

- you want to generate more cash flow in your life;
- you are raising money for a special purpose, occasion or purchase; or
- you would like to be more aware of the flow of abundance and prosperity through your life in general.

Stories About Wealth and Prosperity Bagua in Action

FOUNTAIN OF FORTUNE

Elaine considered herself extremely fortunate to actually be able to buy a home in the affluent neighborhood she'd always wanted to live in. The family who had previously owned the house had gone bankrupt, which had dropped the house into her price range. Although the house had many appealing features, she noticed it didn't "feel" right. She knew the previous owners had experienced a great deal of monetary stress there. She asked me to take a brief look at the house before she moved her furniture in, and then to return to help her set up the interior when all her possessions arrived.

One look at her new L-shaped house, with its Wealth area located in a swampy spot in the backyard, let me know that there were some important Bagua enhancements needed. We discussed the possibility of extending the existing deck out to square off the house—a major project, and one

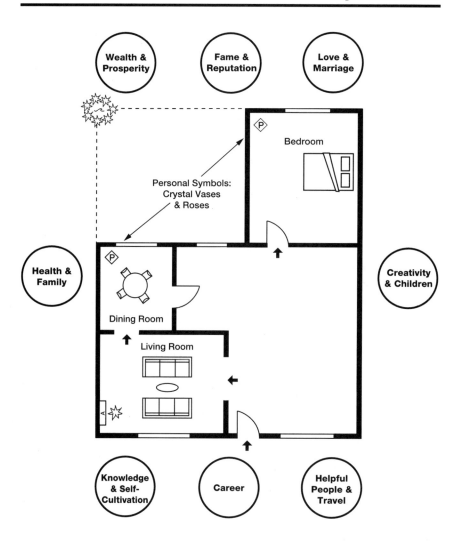

Wealth & Prosperity

Fame & Reputation

Love & Marriage

Personal Symbols:
Crystal Vases
& Roses

Bedroom

Health & Family

Creativity & Children

Dining Room

Living Room

Knowledge & Self-Cultivation

Career

Helpful People & Travel

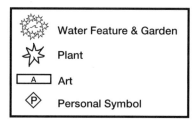

Water Feature & Garden

Plant

Art

Personal Symbol

Fountain of Fortune

she could not afford for at least a year. Still, we knew something needed to be done immediately to change the "bankrupting" shape of the house.

Treatments and Results:

I suggested a large water feature in the Wealth area to symbolically square off the house, and to lift and circulate the Ch'i. This suited Elaine just fine, and over the next week while the house was being painted, she installed a five-foot fountain with an angel figure at the top, and surrounded the base with a raised bed of red, blue, and violet flowers. As soon as she moved her furniture in, we met again and went through the house to enhance the Prosperity areas in all the rooms. She looked through her art, vases, and crystal, chose the pieces that inspired feelings of wealth and abundance, and placed them in the Wealth areas in each room. She kept a crystal vase of fresh red roses in the Wealth area of her bedroom, symbolizing both prosperity and love. To complete her treatment, she hung a wind chime by the front door to "call in wealth and auspicious opportunities."

The Ch'i of Elaine's new house was transformed when we were finished. To keep the Ch'i circulating, I suggested that she leave her fountain on all the time for a while, and light it so that it could be seen at night.

After four years, Elaine continues to enjoy the sight and sound of her Bagua "Wealth Garden." Unlike the previous owners, her finances have steadily grown. New opportunities to increase her wealth continually flow into her life, securing her financial health and well-being.

▼▼▼

VELVETEEN BATHROOMS

Helena knew right away when she rented her condo that it needed some Feng Shui assistance. The first of the three levels consisted of a small dark foyer, a stairway to the second floor, and doors to the outside, the garage, and the coat closet. Although she didn't know exactly why, Helena had a funny feeling about the location of the condo's two bathrooms. As it turned out, they were located in the Wealth areas on both the second and third floors.

Treatments and Results:

To keep the house's Ch'i from "pouring out the door," I suggested that she hang a round faceted crystal high above the bottom stair, and install a wardrobe mirror on the coat closet door. Both of these objects would help to lift and circulate the Ch'i back into the upper stories of the condo. I instructed her to hang the crystal at least seven feet above the stair, so that no one felt as if they would run into it. Also, I asked her to hang the wardrobe mirror high enough on the closet door so that she and her friends could see their entire heads when looking into it. The mirror would also enlarge and brighten the foyer.

"To really keep the Ch'i uplifted, hang art that you are very attracted to on the stairway wall," I suggested. "It should make your heart sing every time you see it. Be sure not to hang your art in a descending pattern that follows the stairs. Choose pieces large enough to hang on their own, or form a horizontal line with several pieces."

Upstairs, to keep Helena's prosperity from "pouring down the drain," we talked about the importance of closing the drains in the bathrooms when they were not in use. Helena decided she was going to keep her sink and shower drains closed, as well as keep her toilet lid down.

"Ch'i flows very much like water, and has a tendency to be pulled down any open drain, especially an opening as big as a toilet," I said.

"None of my vital Ch'i is going to be sucked out of my house!" she insisted.

She was serious. The day after our appointment, she installed the mirror and crystal in the foyer. Even though she was renting her home, Helena decided to replace the old corroded drain in the bathtub of her master bath with a new one that she could easily open and close. She made plans to decorate both of her baths in rich velveteen colors with elegant brass accessories.

Two days after our appointment, Helena received a check that she had been promised for over a year. She was stunned that it arrived right after she had placed her Bagua crystal and mirror in the foyer. It could be a coincidence, she thought, or it could be a sign that her Wealth Ch'i was really circulating. She made an appointment with a plumber to replace the tub drain, and began to embellish both bathrooms with the colors and accessories that made her feel rich and luxurious. Three days after the drain replacement was complete. Helena received a substantial check from her parents' trust—a fund that had supposedly been emptied months ago. She called me immediately to report the good news.

"This is amazing," she exclaimed. "I had no idea Feng Shui could produce such lucrative results!"

"Your willingness to make your home the very best it can be has everything to do with it," I said. "When you sculpt the Ch'i to flow harmoniously around you, beautiful things happen—in your case, beautiful money things!"

NEW HOME, NEW CHOICES

I met Sandy for the first time when she asked me to take a look at the house she was trying to sell. It had been nothing but trouble to her, with leaks and mold and now, bad memories. Her marriage had ended in this house. Now, she and her young daughter wanted to make a fresh start in another house.

Her driveway was on a steep downhill grade, putting the house far below street level and into perpetual shade. I surveyed the overall shape of the house and found that it was missing both the Wealth area and the Love and Marriage area, with the Fame and Reputation area jutting like a peninsula into the backyard.

"I bet you have a great reputation at work and in the community," I ventured.

Sandy looked at me a bit startled. " Why yes, I think so. I'm very active with a local charity, and I know I have a good reputation at work. Why?"

I pointed out to her that the Fame and Reputation area was represented by the covered porch in the back of her house, while the Wealth area sat in the middle of the back patio, and the Marriage area was on a rough downhill slope in the backyard.

"Wouldn't you just know," she frowned. "No wonder my finances are always strained. I spend money faster than I make it, and it's usually on this house! And Love and Marriage, I don't even want to talk about that. So now, what should I do about it? I just want to sell this house and get out of here."

We spent the next hour planning enhancements for the two missing areas. For the Wealth area, we decided that several large containers of bright flowers and palms would be enough to secure and stabilize the Wealth Ch'i. In the Love area, the installation of a large raised bird feeder would bring in the enlivening Ch'i of wildlife, while ferns and shade-loving flowers would brighten the area. Sandy realized that she needed to install proper steps in the area so that people could safely walk to and from the lower part of the property.

To lift the Ch'i of the low-lying location, I suggested that Sandy make two additions to the roof of her house. One was a prominent weathervane that included the shape of a bird, and the other was lights that illuminated the four main corners of the roof. The landscaping along the walkway to the front door needed massive plantings of yellow and red flowers to bring in the Earth and Fire elements, lift the Ch'i and balance the swampy wet feeling of the land. This would also help balance the recessed location of the house, and attract the right buyer.

A week later, Sandy and I met again to view the two houses she was considering for purchase. One was ruled out immediately due to its overwhelming Feng Shui challenges. The other was particularly interesting to me. It was exactly the same shape as the house she was selling. Although it was built at street level, it too was missing the Wealth and the Love Bagua areas, while the Fame and Reputation area jutted out in the back as a room addition. Sandy was in love with the positive aspects of the house—location, view, and general ambiance—and wanted to resolve the Bagua problems it presented.

"I want to make this house work. What do I need to do?"

We took a detailed look around. Much of the back of the house had been decked so that the Love area was minimally defined by the deck's structure. However, the Wealth area had not been included when the deck had been built, leaving it out on an extreme slope down into a canyon.

"This reminds me of the Wealth area in the house you're selling," I said.

"That's totally unacceptable," said Sandy. "I will not have my finances roll down any hill! What do I do to fix it?"

Treatments and Results:

We came up with a viable plan. First, Sandy was going to have to build up and terrace the hill so that there was even ground to work with. Next, the ground would need to be bricked, bringing in the stabilizing influence of solid Earth, and securing a place for an outdoor water fountain, pots of flowers, and a bench. Sandy needed to find a fountain she loved that was at least five feet high to stabilize the Wealth area. The bench would be added to draw people to her Wealth area and invite them to linger.

For several weeks after our appointment, Sandy shopped and shopped for the perfect fountain. Finally, she found the right one and had it installed on her newly built brick patio. Two days later, she realized the biggest financial gain she'd ever had. She was shocked, and told me on the phone that it almost scared her.

"You didn't tell me it would work so fast!" she exclaimed.

"Well, I never know for sure what's going to happen," I said. "I do know that if you enhance any Bagua area in just the right way, you'll get results quickly."

Sandy was quiet for a minute, then said, "I'm going to leave my Love area alone for a while. I'm not ready to see what happens when I start enhancing that one!"

Personalized Enhancements for Wealth and Prosperity

Choose one or a combination of the following things to personally enhance your Wealth and Prosperity area.

- Items that "call in the Ch'i," such as wind chimes, wind socks, whirligigs, and flags
- Valuable possessions and collections, such as antiques, art, sculpture, coins, and crystal
- Posters, paintings, collages, photos, and figures that depict desired possessions such as homes, cars, boats, equipment, jewelry; and that give a strong feeling of wealth and abundance
- Items in the colors of blue, purple, and red
- Healthy plants, especially with shiny, rounded, coin-shaped leaves, such as jade, impatiens, and begonia; plants that bloom in the Wealth colors of reds, purples, and blues, such as gloxinia, cyclamen, begonia, African violet, kalanchoe, and mums
- Fresh and silk flowers in reds, purples, and blues
- Water features, such as fountains and waterfalls, symbolizing the abundant flow of money and prosperity
- Quotes, affirmations, and sayings pertaining to Wealth and Prosperity

- Things that have a personal association to Wealth and Prosperity, such as the dollar bill earned in a new business, foreign money brought back from a successful trip, etc.

Affirmations for Wealth and Prosperity

Choose any of the affirmations below that you feel an affinity for, write them down, and place them in the Wealth and Prosperity area of your home, office, room, desk or any other Bagua area you are working with. Or, use these affirmations as a guide in creating your own personal affirmations for wealth, abundance, and prosperity.

I am rich and prosperous in every way.

There is a generous flow of wealth and prosperity in my life.

The finest riches of health, wealth, and happiness are constantly blossoming in my life.

Wealth and prosperity manifest easily and joyfully into my life, now and always.

I am blessed with a constant and abundant flow of money in my life.

The Bagua Map
FAME AND REPUTATION

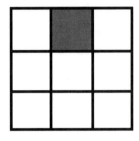

Your Fame and Reputation area is located at the back of the structure you are working with, midway between Wealth and Prosperity, and Love and Marriage. (See the Bagua Map, page 62.)

The I Ching's Wisdom on Fame and Reputation

Fame and Reputation are associated with *Li*, the I Ching trigram meaning "Clinging Fire." One of the attributes of Fire is that it clings to whatever it is burning—a natural condition that also applies to our reputation in the community. Whether good or bad, our reputation is impossible to simply shake off. It clings tight, either warming or burning us in the hearts and minds of others. When we cultivate a good reputation, friendly relations spring up all around us, setting up the best chances for a secure and happy future. When we live interdependently, giving and receiving support and assistance, a good reputation is assured. This opens our world to the synergistic connections and auspicious opportunities that occur only when trust and fair play are in place. Our life is "illuminated" with good will. Simply put, building good relations in our community is the intelligent thing to do. If we choose to "burn our bridges," and pay no attention to creating a positive reputation with friends and community, our future is jeopardized. Eventually, we could find ourselves distrusted and alone, and therefore, unsupported and uncared for. The I Ching reminds us to be mindful of what we are famous for—it's only natural that it will cling to us for a long time.

▼▼▼

Enhance your Fame and Reputation areas when:

- you would like more recognition at work or at home;
- you want to establish a good reputation in your community; or
- you would like to be well known for something you do.

Stories About Fame and Reputation Bagua in Action

MIRROR, MIRROR, ON THE WALL...

Lee had lived with her 12-year-old son in a small cottage surrounded by farmland for about a year. Most of her life was great. Her son did very well in school, they enjoyed many creative projects together, and her health was excellent. But, as a brilliant technical writer, she knew she should be enjoying more opportunities to participate in interesting projects. Instead, her employer seemed to have forgotten how talented she was, and gave her work that was well below her skill level. She had recently applied for employment in several other companies, and even with samples of her best work in hand, no one seemed to be interested. "Before we moved to this house, there was no end to my writing opportunities," Lee told me. "Please come over and tell me what's happened!"

As soon as I arrived, I noticed that Lee's little home was a perfect rectangle. There was a cozy feeling throughout the rooms, with many photographs of loved ones on walls and shelves. It was only when we got to the bathroom, exactly in the Fame and Reputation area, that I understood the problem. Unlike the rest of the house, the bathroom needed many repairs. Peeling wallpaper and dark watermarks scarred the walls. A strong moldy smell filled the air. But what was most urgently in need of change was the placement of a medicine cabinet mirror. It had been hung low over the toilet, so that as I looked into it, it cut my image off at my chest. I asked Lee to stand in front of it. Her image was perfectly severed at her throat.

"Do you use this mirror?" I asked.

"Oh, yes, I just stoop to see myself in it." As Lee spoke, her eyes got wide with sudden realization. "You don't mean my having to stoop low every day to see myself has anything to do with...oh my gosh, how do we fix it?!"

Treatments and Results:

Lee got a towel and draped the medicine cabinet to cover the mirror. The Ch'i in the room immediately changed for the better. I suggested that she take the cabinet down and replace it with art that personally symbolized Fame and Reputation to her. She imagined a photograph of elegant paper and pens in a bright red frame. I also suggested that she replace both floor and wall coverings as soon as possible, remembering that red accents in the Fame area are always great. After all, this was her "Hall of Fame," and it needed to be filled with warm and lively Ch'i. I reminded her to keep the toilet lid down, and to consider closing the sink and shower drains when not in use, so as not to "drain" the Ch'i. Next, we talked about lighting. The one overhead lamp left the existing mirror over the sink in semi-darkness. She decided to install track lights directly over the mirror and to enjoy standing up straight in front of it each day.

Lee transformed the bathroom over the next two weeks. As she worked on it, she kept realizing how "small" she'd begun to feel, stooping in dim light in front of a tiny low mirror every day. She decided to make a collage of photographs of herself working with other people, frame it in red, and hang it where the medicine cabinet had been. She replaced the rug, removed the wallpaper, painted the walls glossy white, and bought new red towels. She also installed three petite track lights to illuminate the mirror over the sink. Several weeks later, a wonderful opportunity came "out of the blue." Lee was hired to design and write a curriculum for a progressive private school—a project that was both lucrative and challenging to her. While working on the curriculum, she met people who recognized her talent and hired her for another educational project. Lee had found her niche, and her reputation as a technical writer was back on track.

▼▼▼

TOO MUCH OF A GOOD THING

Sharon called me because a friend suggested that Feng Shui might help her with her dilemma. Apparently, the more famous she got, the unhappier her husband Al became. It had gotten to the point where their 20-plus-year marriage was feeling very strained.

"He says if I'd just make some decent money while I'm getting all this attention, he'd be happier," she lamented as we visited before taking our Feng Shui walk through the house.

"What are you becoming so famous for?" I asked.

"California cuisine," she answered. "I have written several cookbooks and am constantly invited to do book signings and radio talk shows. Plus, I teach cooking classes here at the house. That's why we remodeled the kitchen."

My Feng Shui warning light went on. "Let's take a look at your kitchen," I suggested.

We walked through their extensive kitchen. Sure enough, their previously rectangular home had been popped out in the Fame and Reputation area with the kitchen remodel. This left the Wealth and Prosperity area and the Love and Marriage areas recessed, with no literal or symbolic structure holding them in place.

I explained what I saw. Sharon looked very annoyed. "I knew we should have enlarged the whole back of the house, but there didn't seem to be a good reason, and it would have been much more expensive. As it stands now, I've yet to do as well financially since we remodeled as I did before! People hear me or see me somewhere, and then want to take my class for a discount, or for free. I hear more sob stories!"

"Your house is now supporting your Fame and Reputation, not your pocketbook, and people are responding in kind," I commented. "This actually can be easy to adjust. You and your husband just need to strengthen the two areas left outside when you extended the kitchen."

Al joined us, and we discussed all the possible options. They immediately liked the idea of filling in the Wealth and the Love areas with simple cement patios and overhead arbors. The kitchen addition already included patio doors out to the lawn. Now, the doors would lead to outdoor patio "rooms" instead. The arbors overhead would provide some structural solidity, necessary shade, and a place to grow flowering vines. I suggested that they plant two identical vines in the Love area that produced a fragrant bloom such as jasmine, and let them intertwine up the arbor. In the Wealth area, vines that bloomed in purple or red would be best.

We looked around the rest of their home. In general, it was gracious and orderly, with the Ch'i flowing harmoniously from room to room.

The master bedroom was done entirely in blue, with dark wooden furniture. Their room of rest and intimacy was dominated by the Wood element, and cast a palpable coolness over everything. I suggested that they introduce some warm pastels such as peach, pink, or apricot, strengthening the Metal and Fire elements, and elementally balancing the room. They could start right away with new linens and round accent pillows in warm tones to heat it up a bit, then consider painting the walls in a warm tone, as well.

We ended our session by looking at the paintings that they had in the living room. Clearly, they both loved their choices and were happy to tell me all about the circumstances that led them to each one. As I left, I noticed that Al had his arm around Sharon. Good sign.

Treatments and Results:

Al took on the patio project with a vengeance, and had it scheduled and built within a month. He and Sharon planted their vines and dressed the patios up with potted plants and simple outdoor furniture. Shortly thereafter, Al's work took a surprising turn. He was offered a lucrative promotion that required him to move to work in another city for six months. I talked to Sharon during this time. She was thoroughly enjoying her husband's temporary relocation.

"He comes home almost every weekend, and it's like a honeymoon. Our love life hasn't been this good in years! During the week, we're both busy." Sharon chatted on and on. "I have my cooking classes here in the evenings without interfering with his life. It's really quite wonderful. And I've transformed the bedroom into our weekend love nest. You'll be happy to know there's almost no blue left in there, literally or figuratively."

Personalized Enhancements for Fame and Reputation

Choose one or a combination of the following items to personally enhance your Fame and Reputation areas:

- Diplomas, awards, prizes, and acknowledgments
- Things made from animals, such as leather, feathers, wool, and bone
- Posters, paintings, collages, photos; and figures of animals, people, fire, sunshine, favorite celebrities
- Items in the red color spectrum
- Triangular, conical, and pyramidal shaped items
- All pleasant lighting, including sunlight, candles, electrical lights, oil lamps
- Quotes, affirmations, and sayings pertaining to Fame and Reputation
- Things that have a personal association to Fame and Reputation, such as awards, diplomas, trophies, etc.

Affirmations for Fame and Reputation

I am honored and respected in every way by the people I work with, and for the work that I do.

I enjoy an abundance of support and enthusiasm for my accomplishments from the people in my community.

I am well known and well respected for my skills, talents, and accomplishments.

My reputation for honesty, trustworthiness, and compassion grows with each passing day.

▼▼▼

The Bagua Map
LOVE AND MARRIAGE

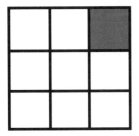

Your Love and Marriage Bagua area is in the rear right section of the structure you are working with. (See the Bagua Map, page 62.)

The I Ching's Wisdom on Love and Marriage

Love and Marriage are under the domain of *K'un*, the I Ching trigram translated as the "Receptive Earth." As the most yin, or yielding, of all the trigrams, K'un is associated with adaptability, devotion, and unconditional support—qualities that we find in true love and happy marriages. Love relationships thrive on the dance of responsive yielding—each partner supporting and allowing the other to fully develop and express themselves. The I Ching teaches that when BOTH partners support, trust, and yield to the other partner's path, there is a loving comfort that blesses the relationship and assures happiness.

The same nurturing, supportive stance is taken when you fully love *yourself*. You take the time to listen to what you need and then gladly give it to yourself, whether it's a hot bath, enrollment in college, or a weekend camping trip in the woods. You get out of your own way and willingly receive from the one person you know intimately from birth to death—YOU.

Enhance your Love and Marriage areas when:

- you would like to attract a love relationship;
- you want to improve the love relationship you have now; or
- you are developing or improving a healthy, happy relationship with yourself.

Love and Marriage Bagua in Action

LOVE LIGHT

Donna and Jay were roommates who shared the same dilemma. Neither one seemed to be able to get a date! They were both attractive and willing to meet new people, but every time either of them met a potential partner, something happened.

"I found out he's married...."

"She told me she's engaged...."

"He's dating three other women, and one of them is my good friend!"

"She was waiting for her boyfriend when we met...." Their stories of ill-fated meetings went on and on.

Interestingly enough, Donna had originally bought her home with her ex-husband. They had decided to add a master bedroom suite, and less than a year after the room was complete, they had separated. They didn't know that by reshaping their home into an L, they had radically changed the shape of the house and affected the Bagua. The Love and Marriage area was relegated to the backyard, with no structure such as a porch or covered deck to support it.

Donna turned pale as I explained to her that the house was missing the Bagua area associated with Love and Marriage. "You don't suppose that's why my marriage didn't..." Her sentence trailed off.

"It could have been a contributing factor," I said. "Now, let's do everything we can to balance and strengthen the area, and see what happens to your love life."

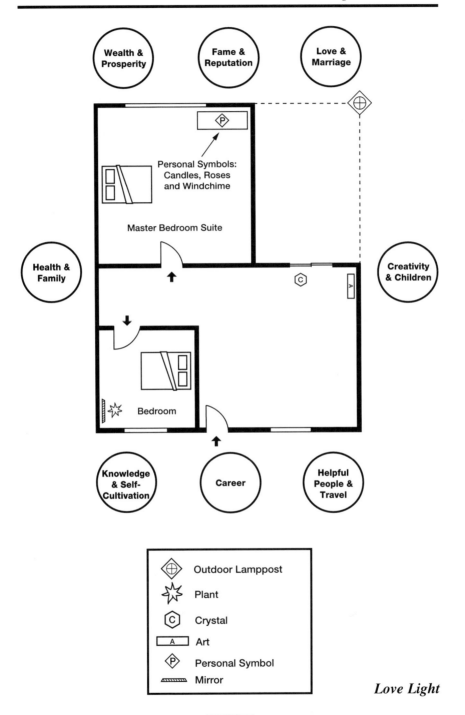

Wealth & Prosperity

Fame & Reputation

Love & Marriage

Personal Symbols: Candles, Roses and Windchime

Master Bedroom Suite

Health & Family

Creativity & Children

Bedroom

Knowledge & Self-Cultivation

Career

Helpful People & Travel

⊕ Outdoor Lamppost

☆ Plant

Ⓒ Crystal

[A] Art

⟨P⟩ Personal Symbol

≈≈≈ Mirror

Love Light

Treatments and Results:

Donna's budget was too small for major enhancements, so she decided to install a standard outdoor lamppost in the corner where the house would have extended had it been square. Fortunately, Jay had the skills and the enthusiasm to do the installation. I suggested that once the light was installed, it should be kept on all the time to "light up" and lift the collapsed Ch'i.

Inside, Donna and Jay had an abstract poster in the dining room's Love area suggesting a sad-looking man in dark yellows and browns. I asked if they liked the piece. It was Jay's, and he'd never thought about whether he liked it or not. Now that he really looked at it, he realized it conveyed a feeling of loneliness and sadness.

"It's part of my past, but it certainly doesn't belong in my future!" He took it down immediately, much to Donna's relief.

I suggested that they enhance the area with romantic art that they both really liked, as well as hanging a round faceted crystal in a nearby east window to catch the morning sun and circulate the Ch'i.

I requested that Donna and Jay think about what objects symbolized Love and Marriage to each of them. Two of Donna's symbols were candles and fresh flowers. She decided that she would set up a table with red and pink candles and fresh roses in the Love and Marriage area of her bedroom. She had always loved the sound of wind chimes, and decided to hang a beautiful set above her "love" table to call in the Ch'i.

"I'm going to buy myself roses in my favorite colors every week, even after I meet the love of my life!" she said.

Jay wasn't immediately sure what symbolized Love to him. He looked a little lost, so we made some suggestions, and he said he'd think about it for a few minutes. In the meantime, Jay showed me his room. It was a disaster area. Packed boxes piled high in the Love area gave the room a storeroom appearance. His only furniture was a futon on the floor with papers and clothes piled all around it. Obviously, Jay's room needed more than a romantic enhancement or two. We sketched out a master plan, including purchases of basic furniture, and bed placement.

"You want to see the door from your bed, but not be directly in front of it, the way your futon is now," I advised. "Begin by moving your bed over and taking the boxes out of your Love and Marriage area. Then, when inspiration strikes, enhance your Love area. You'll know exactly what to do."

They set to work, and within a week, the lamp post was installed and shining brightly in the Love area outside. Jay slid his futon over to a more favorable location and moved his boxes into the garage to be unpacked there. He'd been mulling over what symbolized love and romance to him when he came upon a forgotten heirloom, an ornately framed mirror that had belonged to his grandparents. They were certainly a great example of love, having been happily married for over 50 years. He hung up the mirror and added a healthy palm that reminded him of romantic getaways. Meanwhile, Donna's candles, roses, and wind chimes were all arranged, and she was in search of the perfect dining room art.

It was eight days after our appointment that Donna heard from an attractive single man she'd met at a party about three months before. He had just found her number after all this time and wanted to know if she would like to take a walk on the beach Saturday? Yes! She was so happy, she ran outside and danced around the light post like it was a Maypole.

"The Ch'i is moving!" she exclaimed.

Jay didn't have to wait long either. He ran into an old flame while grocery shopping, and the fire seemed to rekindle between them on the spot. He tells the story, all smiles, of being questioned by the police when he and his new/old love were found "necking" on the beach.

And it didn't stop there. A month later, Donna was getting so much attention from several men that she decided to turn the "love light" off during the day. Jay was captivated by his sweetheart and she turned out to be a great help to him as they "Feng Shui-ed" his bedroom together.

When I talked to Donna recently, she said that Jay and his girlfriend had decided to get their own place, and she was planning to move to another state with her fiancé. We both chuckled when she reminded me that they never did get any new art for the dining room. They'd decided that they better not bring any more romance Ch'i into the house!

▼▼▼

TIME FOR LOVE

Jenny was frustrated with her love life. "My romantic relationships just don't seem to last," she sighed. "I'm about to tell the guy I'm dating that I don't want to see him anymore because it's just not working."

Jenny lived in a beautiful two-story condominium that had a large living room graciously decorated with a mix of contemporary and antique furnishings. In the Love and Marriage area stood the fireplace.

"Would you say your relationships are like quick, hot fires that don't last long?" I asked.

"Well, sort of," she replied. "They usually start off pretty lively, then they just seem to wind down, and I lose interest...."

I studied the objects that Jenny had placed on the mantel. There were two identical topiaries made of dried flowers that were quite beautiful. They stood like sentinels at either end. In the middle, dominating most of the mantel, was a broken antique clock made of a sizable chunk of black marble.

"How long has your clock been out of order?" I asked.

"Oh, it's never worked, even after one repairman thought he'd fixed it. I keep saying I'm going to take it to someone, but it's so heavy and awkward, I haven't done it."

I explained to Jenny that the fireplace was in her Love

and Marriage area, then asked her to stand in front of the mantel and tell me what she saw. She said sardonically, "I see two people separated by something that's not working. Isn't that just terrific!?"

Treatments and Results:

Jenny marched up to the mantel and, with a lot of effort, pushed the clock to one side. She then took the topiaries and centered them together so that their pots and foliage were touching. She stepped back to view her handiwork.

"Wow, that makes a difference, but that clock's going to have to go," she said. Before I could help her, she had muscled the clock off the mantel. As she did so, the clock began to chime. Jenny's face showed complete shock and amazement. "It's never worked before!" she whispered, as the clock chimed away in her arms. She lowered it onto a table and stared first at *it*, then at me.

"What does this mean?" she asked, as the chimes continued.

"What does it mean to you, Jenny?" I asked.

Covered with goosebumps, her eyes wide, she said, "I think it's high time I fixed this clock. It's been the symbol of how my relationships work!"

We looked at the rest of her home. In her bedroom, Jenny had a silk flower arrangement in the Love area. Prominent in the arrangement were two roses, one faced in one direction, and the other faced in the opposite direction. When I pointed this out to her, she immediately pulled them out, intertwined them so that they were facing each other, and put them back. Also in the bedroom. there were two teddy bears, one on the bed, and one on the chair. I suggested that she place them together in her den's Love and Marriage area as whimsical additions to her bookshelf. The bears in her bedroom were symbols of someone already being in her boudoir, leaving no room for a new lover. I also suggested that she buy new sheets in a warm flesh tone such as pink, peach, or apricot, to signal a new beginning in her love life. I suggested that Jenny put pairs of things such as candles and flowers everywhere she wanted, especially in her Love and Marriage areas. They would enhance the Ch'i and serve as environmental affirmations, reminding her that her true love was close at hand.

We surveyed Jenny's den. On her desk stood another antique clock that didn't work—right in the Love and Marriage area of the desk! We looked even closer. Below the face of the clock was a picture of a forlorn-looking woman.

"Do you even believe this?" she cried. "Another dead clock, and look at this woman. She reminds me of me!" She grabbed the clock from the desk and put it behind her back. We both started to laugh.

"There's no place to hide from Feng Shui eyes," I said.

The next day, Jenny took her clocks in for repair. When they were working again, she placed the large black one in the career area of her den. She replaced the picture in the smaller one with one of a couple, and put it on her mantel. She further enhanced her mantel with a pair of crystal candlesticks, and a small oil painting of hearts.

After all her enhancements were in place, Jenny decided to have a party. On the night of her celebration, one of her good friends called to ask if her brother Jason could come to the party, also. Three guesses what happened. Jason and Jenny hit it off immediately. His comment to her was, "This is very timely. I was just thinking about how I'd like to meet someone special, and here you are...."

Nipping It in the Bud

Meg and David had been married for less than a year. They had cheerfully given up their tiny apartment for the chance to own a house, even though it was a "fixer-upper."

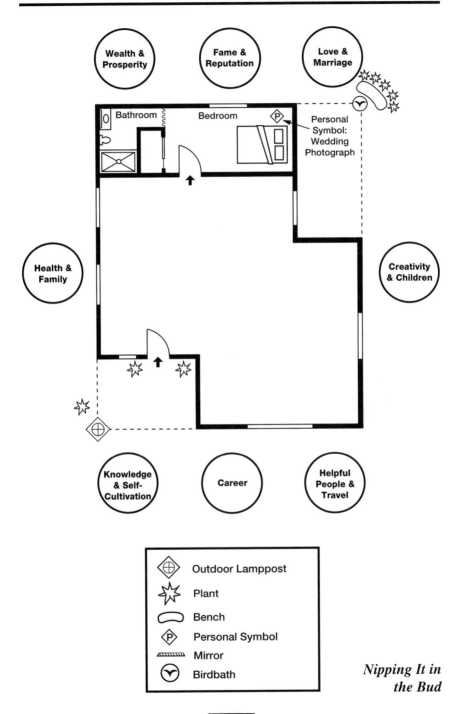

Nipping It in the Bud

Meg was suspicious that the house had "bad Feng Shui" because the previous owner had been divorced several times while living there. She asked for a consultation and blessing.

A fixer-upper it was. The house stood out in their neighborhood as the one with "no yard." Only the hardiest weeds grew in the exposed, chalky subsoil. The garage protruded from the house, leaving the Knowledge and Self-Cultivation area and the Love and Marriage area outside of the structure. We all agreed that there was some work to be done to balance and enhance the Ch'i.

Treatments and Results:

We talked at length about how to enhance the two missing areas. The Knowledge area was at the edge of a front patio and could be included in the structure by enlarging the existing overhead arbor. Since the front needed lighting, I suggested that Meg and David begin their enhancements immediately by installing a lamppost in the corner to "light up" the Ch'i of Knowledge and Self-Cultivation. Pots of bright flowers around the lamp, as well as near the door, would enliven the sluggish Ch'i even further. I also asked the couple to remove all dead plants from the yard, even if they weren't going to do anything else with it for a while. This would begin the process of renewal and improve the Ch'i as it meandered over waiting soil, rather than a plant graveyard.

The Love and Marriage area of the house was relegated to a bare patch of ground in the backyard. It was the last place anyone would want to go. No windows looked out upon it, nor did the rest of the yard seem to include it. I asked David and Meg to think about what they would like to put there that would have substance and structure, as well as romantic meaning. David immediately saw as their outdoor retreat area, beginning with a bench, where they could talk and watch the sunsets in the evenings. Meg thought it was a great place to have a nature sanctuary, including a birdbath.

David suddenly realized he could plant his rose garden there, something he had wanted to do for years, but hadn't had the land to cultivate until now. I suggested that they find a large birdbath that they both loved and install it on the "missing" corner, then spread out from there. The more beauty they created together, the better!

Inside, the master bedroom also needed help. There was only one place for the bed to go, and it faced the bathroom. Meg's view from her side of the bed was through the open dressing area to a distant mirror over the bathroom sink. David's view was directly into a mirrored closet door.

"My prediction is that if you live with this for a while, you will never share the same point of view," I said.

"That's already started to happen!" exclaimed Meg. "We were just talking about how we've been arguing much more since we moved in here."

I suggested that they curtain the open entrance to the bathroom area, and either panel the mirrored closet doors with the same fabric, or install plain doors. I explained that mirrors do not belong across from people's beds. Their vital Ch'i would be depleted if they scared themselves in the middle of the night by seeing their own movement. And, in Meg and David's case, there were plenty of mirrors to see themselves in the bath area. I also suggested that they choose a personal symbol of their relationship to put on Meg's side of the bed in the Love and Marriage area of the room. Meg immediately envisioned their favorite wedding photograph there. Perfect.

Soon after our appointment, David went on a business trip overseas, and brought back two bolts of creamy raw silk. While he was gone, Meg had the mirrored closet doors replaced with wooden ones. When David returned, they made simple curtains and hung them in front of the dressing area entrance. The room became much cozier and inviting, and they noticed that their bickering ceased. David installed a bright outdoor light in the Knowledge area, and a new birdbath and bench in the Love and Marriage area.

As spring rolled around, David made his fantasy rose

garden into a beautiful reality. He shaped the beds into a soft arc "to embrace the house, the bench, and us!," as he put it. David and Meg nipped the house's Feng Shui problems in the bud, and as they continue to improve their home, they are enjoying the harmonious Ch'i that envelops them.

Personalized Enhancements for Love and Marriage

You can choose one or a combination of items from this list to personally enhance your Love and Marriage area:

- Posters, paintings, collages, photos, and figures of your significant other
- Pairs of things, such as lovers, doves, dolphins, hearts, etc.; symbols of love
- Items in the colors of red, pink, and white
- Quotes, affirmations, and sayings pertaining to Love and Marriage
- Things that have a personal association to Love and Marriage, such as romantic vacation and honeymoon mementos, anniversary gifts, etc.

▼▼▼

Affirmations for Love and Marriage

Choose affirmations from the list below that you are attracted to, write them down, and place them in the Love and Marriage area in your home, bedroom, on your bureau, or in any other Love and Marriage area you are working with. Or, you can use the affirmations here to guide you in writing your own personal affirmations.

I attract joy, love, and intimacy into my life.

I love, respect, and honor myself.

Love constantly surrounds me.

I love to love and be loved.

I am a beautiful, loving, joyful person.

My love partner and I experience an abundance of joy, passion, and ecstasy together.

My perfect love partner and I are connected in our minds, hearts, and spirits, now and always.

The Bagua Map
CHILDREN AND CREATIVITY

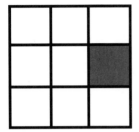

Your Children and Creativity Bagua area is located on the right side of the structure you are working with, midway between Helpful People and Travel in the front, and Love and Marriage in the rear. (See the Bagua Map, page 62.)

The I Ching's Wisdom on Children and Creativity

The I Ching trigram, *Tui,* means "Joyous Lake," and is associated with the qualities of pleasure, generosity, and encouragement. The essential idea of this teaching is that by encouraging others to fully express themselves, we bring success and pleasure to ourselves. Parents sometimes experience this energizing and almost magical satisfaction while encouraging their children to learn and grow through creative expression. The same holds true with our own creativity. We need generous amounts of encouragement and admiration, as well as a playful "lightness of being," to unfold and blossom into full creative expression. In all cases, the flowering of creativity is a joyful experience when it occurs through kindness and encouragement.

▼▼▼

Enhance your Children and Creativity areas when:

• you would like to become pregnant;
• you want to be more creative in general;
• you are involved in a creative project;
• you feel creatively blocked;
• you want to explore and develop your inner child qualities; or
• you'd like to improve your relationship with children.

Creativity and Children Bagua in Action

ROOM FOR CREATIVITY

Bonnie was a frustrated graphic artist. She had all the tools of her trade, but only a puny little space to work in. She lived alone in a 2,000-square-foot home that didn't seem to serve her needs very well. It had a huge living room, an adequate dining room, and a small den she used as both an office and a studio. The day before our appointment, she had done her best to organize the den area. Still, it was cramped with furniture, filing cabinets, art tables, and supplies. The overflow had taken over half of the garage, and was threatening to gobble up the other half. I could see immediately that we needed to talk about room usage. Interestingly enough, the large living room was located in the Creativity and Children area of the house. Since Bonnie lived alone, I knew she could choose to arrange the house to suit her needs, even if it was unconventional.

We sat down and talked about her lifestyle. Did she use the living room for entertaining? No. In fact, she and her friends usually ended up sitting around the kitchen table for the duration of their visit. Did she need a formal dining room? No, she rarely used the dining room. As we talked, I could see that she was clearly preoccupied. She kept scowling and looking toward the den.

"What am I going to do about THAT room?" she blurted out, nodding toward the den.

"How about making it into your living room?" I suggested.

"My living room—what in the world would I do with the real living room?" she asked sharply.

"How about turning the 'real living room' into your art studio, and the 'real dining room' into your office," I offered.

Bonnie looked stunned as the possibilities flooded through her mind. "Oh, why didn't I ever think of that? I've been squeezing myself into half of this house, and leaving the other half vacant!"

Treatments and Results:

The more Bonnie thought about the idea of changing the house around, the more excited she got. I suggested that she arrange all her art tables in the middle of the room where she'd have plenty of room to move around each table. There was also a vast amount of wall space for her shelves of supplies. That meant she could have everything related to art in one spacious area, and reclaim her two-car garage. She loved the idea of separating her office furniture, computer, and files from her creative area. We looked at all her furniture, equipment, and supplies, piece by piece, and decided where they would be placed in her new room arrangements.

She wasted no time hiring two men to help her move everything around. Five days later, Bonnie stepped back and saw a different house. Her new studio was an artist's dream-come-true. Large, airy, and very colorful, it looked like creativity itself. Her office was efficiently arranged and gave her a pretty view out to the garden. But, the biggest surprise for Bonnie was the den. She had only known it as a tiny, frustrating space crammed full of too much furniture. Suddenly, it was transformed into a very cozy, attractive living area, where she could relax in the evenings and entertain friends who now wanted to enjoy the coziness of Bonnie's new living room, rather than sit in the kitchen all evening.

With the enhanced flow of creative Ch'i circulating through the house, Bonnie's personal creativity soared. Along with her graphic design work, she began to explore painting and creative writing. She made many discoveries about her own creative process and developed a class on creativity. Soon, groups were gathering in her spacious studio to explore their own creativity through drawing, painting, and journaling.

Today, Bonnie teaches many classes on creativity, sharing techniques that playfully encourage the creative expression in her students, even those who feel that they've been creatively blocked since childhood. She begins each class by saying, "Welcome to a playground that's big enough for all of us to play in. Here, you have plenty of room to let your creativity blossom and grow."

▼▼▼

ROGUES' GALLERY

Before Ellen moved into her new home, she decided to have a Feng Shui consultation. The house was empty, and she wanted to figure out where her things should be placed to encourage and enhance the vibrant flow of Ch'i.

Her home was in a development of attractive duplexes. The street led me past the backs of the houses, each with easy access to a two-car garage. The idea was to conveniently pull in the garage and enter through an interior garage door into the house. The front entrance could be approached only by walking around the house along a beautifully landscaped meandering path. It struck me as lovely and very unusual. Guests would actually have to walk for two minutes before getting to the front door.

"Are you planning on bringing people around to your front door?" I asked.

"Well, I figured when I was expecting someone, I'd just leave the garage door open," Ellen answered. "Why?"

"Your front door is your home's mouth of Ch'i, and your whole house will be nourished when you use it regularly," I said.

We talked about the mental adjustment she and her friends would need to make to use the front door. She realized that guests would enjoy the brief walk through the garden environment. It would provide a moment to relax and take a breather between driving and arriving.

"Consider putting a large birdbath in the front yard to attract wildlife and to represent the flow of water across the front of your property. It will enhance the Ch'i and provide a centerpiece in your view from the living room windows," I suggested.

Inside, the house promised to be a beauty. A large living room would showcase most of her ethnic art collection, while comfortable beige couches, colorful rugs, and an upright piano would complete the picture. It would be a fabulous room to be greeted by.

"Speaking of enhancing the Ch'i," Ellen said, "I want to enhance my creative Ch'i here. I'm hoping you can help me choose which bedroom upstairs to set up as a studio. I've raised my kids, and now I want to take up painting again."

"Well, you're off to a good start just by surrounding yourself with so much art that you love," I said.

We went upstairs and within two minutes, we had chosen the studio. The room was spacious, had a southern exposure for fabulous light, and sat directly in the Creativity and Children area of the house. Ellen was excited that the room had so much positive Ch'i. We discussed how to arrange the furniture. Her desk would be placed at a diagonal so she could see both the door and the window, while having the storage closet behind her. Her easel and paints would be located near the window to take advantage of the light, and there, too, she would be able to see the door. We could both see it in our mind's eye set up and ready to go.

Downstairs beneath her studio, was the laundry room and the entrance into the house from the garage. This was the place where the Ch'i was really in need of a pick-me-up. As it was, the heavy door was on a large spring that made it dangerous for anyone caught in its path. The door opened into a narrow space between a wall and the washer and dryer. The one overhead light could only be switched on from around the corner, nowhere near the garage entry. We discussed what it would be like to fight the door in the dark with a couple of bags of groceries. Bad Feng Shui!

"This is an important part of the house," I said. "You will come and go through here every day, as well as do your laundry here. It's also associated with Children and Creativity, a part of your life you want to develop, not struggle with. I suggest that you take the spring off the door, improve the lighting, and hang something delightful in here that inspires you every time you see it."

Ellen's eyes lit up as she was struck by an idea. "I know what I'll put in here!" she exclaimed. "I'll make it a rogues' gallery of my children and grandchildren. I've got a ton of pictures of them that I love, and this is the perfect place to display them!"

Treatments and Results:

Ellen moved into her home two weeks later. Her new birdbath was one of the first things to be placed out in the front yard. She set up her studio as planned and immediately began sketching the still-life of her move-in process—Workman's Lunch; Unhung Mask; First Bird. She felt immediately at home and creatively inspired. She had the interior garage door spring removed and track lighting installed. Then the fun began. Many of the photos she had of her kids and grandkids had been packed away for years. Now she could go wild hanging up every single one that she loved. When she was done, she had covered the laundry room walls with framed photos.

In a recent conversation, Ellen told me she was happier than she'd ever been. She was blossoming as a painter and having the best time sketching wherever she went.

"You should have seen my son's face when he discovered my rogues' gallery," she said. "He couldn't believe I'd hidden my photos in the laundry room. He thought it was an insult. I explained to him why they were there, and that I got a chance to really see them every day. Now, he's doing the same thing at his house!"

Personalized Enhancements for Children and Creativity

Choose one or a combination of items from the list below to personally enhance your Children and Creativity Bagua area:

- Posters, paintings, collages, photos; and figures of children (actually created by children) that stimulate the creative juices in you
- Supplies used for creating things, such as art, craft, and building materials
- Whimsical items, toys, and stuffed animals
- Items in the colors of white and pastels
- Circular, oval, or arch-shaped items
- Things made of metal—brass, steel, pewter, silver, gold, aluminum, copper, etc.—such as furniture, candle holders, picture frames, figurines, jewelry, and lamps
- Quotes, affirmations, and sayings pertaining to Children and Creativity
- Things that have personal association to Children and Creativity, such as handmade items, memorabilia from your own childhood, etc.

Affirmations for Children and Creativity

Choose affirmations that personally suit you from the list below, write them down, and place them in the Children and Creativity area in your home or workplace, on your art table, or in any Children and Creativity area you are working with. Or, use the affirmations here as a guide to creating your own.

I easily and joyfully express my creativity.

My creativity flows freely as I express who I am.

I am an artistic, talented, one-of-a-kind creative person.

My child/inner child is safe and happy.

I joyfully support my child/inner child in developing and express-ing his/her creativity.

As my destiny unfolds, I trust my inner wisdom to express my cre-ativity in all the ways that are perfect for me.

I joyfully trust my creative urges and allow myself the time and space to express them.

▼▼▼

The Bagua Map
HELPFUL PEOPLE AND TRAVEL

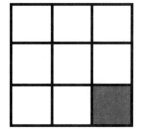

Your Helpful People and Travel area is in the front right section of the structure you are working with. (See the Bagua Map on page 62.)

The I Ching's Wisdom on Helpful People and Travel

Helpful People and Travel are both associated with the I Ching trigram, Ch'ien, meaning "Heaven." As the most yang, or active, of all the trigrams, Heaven has the qualities of power, synchronicity, inspiration, and confidence. Ch'ien reminds us that our lives are shaped by our actions. Right actions come out of the harmonious blending and usage of our intuition and intellect. We know we're on the right track when we experience people as "angels" and places as "paradises." When orchestrated by synchronicity, people and places give us inspiration and guidance, leave benevolent marks upon our life's path, and help us to manifest our destiny. Most of us could relate many stories about how our lives were enhanced or transformed by the words or actions of a mentor, customer, bus driver, employee, or complete stranger. Touched by the Heavenly experience of synchronicity, we suddenly find ourselves standing in the right place at the right time or meeting the right person at just the right moment. It is at those times that we feel the Heavenly forces pressing in closely around us, moving us with grace and ease to the next step.

Enhance your Helpful People and Travel areas when:

- you want to attract more mentors, clients, customers, employees, colleagues—helpful people of any kind—into your life;
- you would like to travel, in general, or go to a specific destination;
- you would like to feel more connected to your spiritual or religious belief system, to the being or beings that you ask to guide you—the ultimate "helpful people"; or
- you are planning to move to a new home or work location.

Helpful People and Travel Bagua in Action

POTTER'S WHEEL OF FORTUNE

Andrea felt like she was drowning in her own success. As a well-known potter, she was inundated with special orders and show deadlines. To produce the amount of pottery she needed to meet her orders, she had hired several employees, but they had proven to be a constant headache. One employee was frequently late, while the others couldn't be trusted to work without constant supervision. To add to her frustration, she had bought a home in another state over a year ago, but one stress-related health problem after another kept her move just out of reach.

"Help!" she cried out to me over the phone.

As I drove up to Andrea's home, I noticed immediately that it was L-shaped, with the Helpful People and Travel area located in the middle of her gravel parking lot. Andrea met me at the door and we toured the house, complete with her studio, extensive outdoor work area, and large kiln. During the tour, I discovered that two of the bathrooms were located in the Health area of the house, neither of which Andrea ever used. One was strictly for the employees, and the other was never used by anyone at all.

Treatments and Results:

Knowing that Andrea was planning on moving in a few months, we looked for something she might already have to put in the missing Helpful People and Travel area to symbolically complete the house. She had a huge potted tree, which we carefully relocated to the exact corner where the house would be if it were square. Around it, we arranged large bricks and other plants to give it even more substance. Then, we checked all the Helpful People areas in each room in the house. I paid special attention to the area where her employees worked. It was clearly a workroom, filled with dusty shelves and drying dishware. I suggested that the Helpful People area be enhanced by the employees, with symbols that were important to them. Andrea readily agreed. I encouraged her to think of ways to bring more Ch'i into the work area. She decided she'd enlarge photographs of her brightly colored finished pottery and hang them in the Career, Wealth, Creativity, and Fame and Reputation areas, lifting the Ch'i and giving the workroom some much-needed splashes of color.

To enhance the Health area, we talked first about simple enhancements for the employee bath. I suggested that she add a healthy plant, some attractive poster art, keep the toilet lid closed, remove the lumber stored under the sink, and give it a thorough cleaning. Then we looked at the unused bathroom. It was large and sunny, with a spotless bathtub and a large closet. It had never occurred to Andrea to use this bathroom herself because it wasn't near her bedroom. She had simply shut it away. I suggested that she enhance her Health Ch'i by making it into a private "getaway" spa where she could relax and rejuvenate after a long day. The idea appealed to her greatly. She had already bought bath accessories for her new home, and decided to get them out and use them in her Health bathroom right away.

In the Health area of her bedroom was a bare wall, scarred with marks from previous artwork. It begged for something beautiful to be put there. Andrea realized she'd taken down a favorite painting when she thought she'd be moving soon and never put it back. Now she would have her lovely painting to look at again when she awoke, not an empty wall.

"Don't pack the things that inspire you too far in advance," I suggested. "Things like your painting keep your Ch'i uplifted and supported, which you especially need through the transitional time of moving."

In the Helpful People and Travel area of her bedroom, I suggested that she hang photographs of her new home to energize her move. She took some photos from a drawer and put them up immediately. I advised her to pack her first official moving box, address it boldly in black ink to her new address, and put it in the Helpful People and Travel area of her living room. "Consider it a piece of art," I said.

Four days later, Andrea called. She was slightly breathless as she recounted what had happened in the last few days. A new employee had literally appeared at her door two days after our appointment, and he had brought two more employable people in since then. The existing employees had appreciated Andrea's offer to personalize their work areas, and had brought in their personal symbols of Helpful People. The workroom's Helpful People area was now alive with images of Mother Mary, Jesus, and a number of saints. Andrea had put up a few color posters of her finished pottery, and with more to come, the workroom was already looking and feeling transformed.

Andrea had decided to use the employee bathroom as a place to experiment with the Bagua. The stored lumber was in the Creativity area, and while removing it, she had found nests of both ants and spiders. She removed them, plugged up the exposed entries, and put a whimsically painted chest there to hold supplies. She placed a new plant in the health area, hung a poster of two folk art doves in the Love area, and put wind chimes in the Wealth area. She had also set up her "spa" bathroom, and had enjoyed a warm bubble bath every night since.

She asked, "What should I do with all these people who

want to work for me? I've gone from too few to too many."

My answer was, "Andrea, let them help you pack!"

▼▼▼

FRONT DOOR WOMAN

The house Amy rented seemed so perfect when she first moved in. It had plenty of space for her at-home business, and for a roommate. Great, except she couldn't seem to find the right person to live with her. Several people had moved in briefly, then moved out again because of some problem, causing the house to feel like it was in a perpetual state of transition. Amy had also noticed that she was having more challenges with her clients. Accounts receivable were mounting up, along with complaints that she felt were unwarranted. Time for some Feng Shui.

Amy's home was in a T shape, missing both the Helpful People and Travel, and the Knowledge and Self-Cultivation areas. The Knowledge area already included a pond, a waterfall, and a pathway to the back door. This area was maintained nicely, and the water feature was a beautiful addition to the property. The Helpful People and Travel area was another issue. It consisted of a pathway that sorely need-ed landscaping leading to the front entrance of the house. Fragments of past landscaping efforts still remained, giving the path a sad, unkempt look. The Feng Shui challenge was definitely in this area.

"Funny," Amy said. "No one ever uses the front door. That's probably why I've let it go so much."

"Why don't you use it?" I asked.

"Because we use the kitchen door to come and go, and my clients come around to the back door, which leads direct-ly into my office."

I knew right away that we would need to circulate more Ch'i through the front entrance. The lack of foot traffic was exacerbating the significant structural imbalance in the

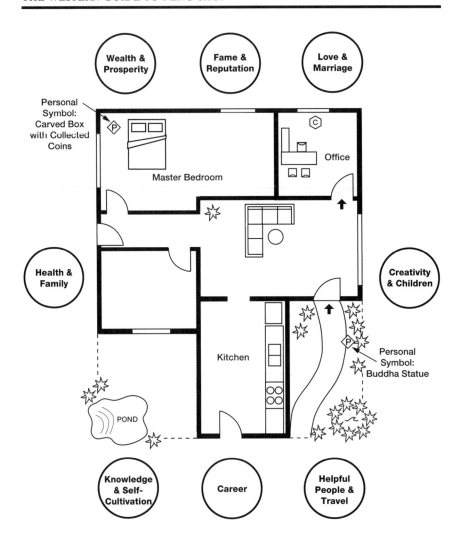

Wealth & Prosperity

Fame & Reputation

Love & Marriage

Personal Symbol: Carved Box with Collected Coins

Master Bedroom

Office

Health & Family

Creativity & Children

Kitchen

Personal Symbol: Buddha Statue

POND

Knowledge & Self-Cultivation

Career

Helpful People & Travel

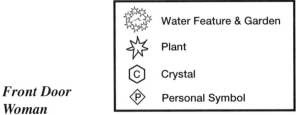

Water Feature & Garden

Plant

Crystal

Personal Symbol

Front Door Woman

Helpful People area. Amy and I discussed the possible enhancements that she could incorporate there. First, the garden needed to be given new life. She also needed to install a lamppost, flagpole, tree, or water fountain to symbolically mark the "missing" corner. And, most importantly, Amy needed to bring her clients in the front door, ushering their Ch'i through the Helpful People and Travel area, and charging it up with activity.

"I suggest that you begin using the front door, also," I said. "Coming in and out of the kitchen door only puts your attention on food. Every time you come home, you immediately think about eating."

Amy laughed. "How did you know? To be on the "Feng Shui diet, I just don't go in the kitchen, right?"

"Well, the Feng Shui diet suggests that you don't continually enter and exit the house through the kitchen," I replied.

As we walked through the house, I noticed that Amy's home was filled with the things she loved. Her color choices and furniture arrangements were all very harmonious. However, she had made the spacious back section of the house, originally the master bedroom, into her office. I could see that she didn't need all the room it provided, and it was located in the most private yin part of the house. Her bedroom was in a smaller room near the front door, which was a more yang location.

"Consider moving your office up to your current bedroom, and your bedroom back to where your office is now. There is too much sleepy Ch'i back there that does not inspire your clients to take you seriously as a businesswoman."

Treatments and Results:

A week after our appointment, Amy installed a beautiful water fountain in her Helpful People and Travel area outside. She took the time to replant and beautify her "helpful people" garden along the pathway leading to the front entrance, incorporating the new fountain and a seated Buddha into her design. Amy also claimed the original master bedroom as her own retreat. Since the Wealth and Prosperity area was located there, she included a beautiful hand-carved box with collected coins on her bureau, calling it her "money magnet."

The room closer to the front door made a lovely and professional-looking office, and it had a much better feeling for work activities. Amy hung a crystal in the window to keep the Ch'i circulating throughout the room. Her clients were ushered into her new office through the front door, where they focused on their appointment, and paid Amy for her services.

A week after Amy installed the water fountain, a friend called "from out of the blue" to say that she was looking for a place to live. Did Amy know of anyone looking for a housemate? Soon, her friend was happily moved in and enhancing the gardens even more with her landscaping skills. Then, Amy's constant reminders to herself to come and go through the front door seemed to produce an unforeseen pay-off. She noticed her focus was less on food and more on fitness. She enrolled in a regular exercise program and found herself really enjoying it.

"Everything seems to be in its rightful place now," she commented recently. "The kitchen is no longer the main thoroughfare, the back retreat is no longer the place of business, the place of business is no longer hidden in the back, and problems with housemates and clients no longer exist."

Personalized Enhancements for Helpful People and Travel

Choose one or a combination of things from the following list to personally enhance the Ch'i in your Helpful People and Travel Bagua areas:

- Posters, paintings, collages, photos; and figures of spiritual

guides, gods, goddesses, saints, and angels
- Helpful people and mentors in your own life
- Special places where you have traveled or want to travel
- Items in the colors of white, gray, and black
- Quotes, affirmations, and sayings pertaining to spiritual guidance, helpful people, and travel
- Things that have a powerful personal association to your spiritual or religious beliefs
- Helpful people such as teachers, mentors, benefactors, clients, customers, and employees
- The places that are special to you in the world

Affirmations for Helpful People and Travel

Choose any of the following affirmations that speak to you, write them down, and place them in the Helpful People and Travel area in your home or workplace, on your desk, or in any other Helpful People and Travel area you are working with. Or, use them as a guide in creating your own personal affirmations.

I constantly attract helpful, generous, loving people into my life.

I am supported and loved by all the people in my life.

I am blessed with many helpful people in my life, and I am a helpful person in other people's lives.

Auspicious opportunities and circumstances are constantly manifesting in my life.

I travel as often as I like, to the places I want to visit.

I am in the right place at the right time, and I meet the right people at the right time.

The Bagua Map
CAREER

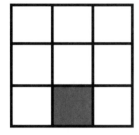

Your Career area is located in the front of the structure you are working with, midway between Knowledge and Self-Cultivation on the left, and Helpful People and Travel on the right. (See Bagua Map on page 62.)

The I Ching's Wisdom on Career

The I Ching trigram, *K'an*, means "Deep Water," and is associated with our life's work or career. For many of us, the greatest challenge in life is discovering and performing the work that we love to do in the world. It's often a deep, mysterious question that can remain unanswered for years, or even a lifetime. It is also a question that can surface at any time in our lives, pulling us inward to contemplate "What's next?" The I Ching instructs us to be completely sincere and diligent in our quest. Being willing to go deep inside ourselves and tell the truth, even when the answer is "I don't know," is crucial. Our sincerity also helps us to maintain clarity and keeps us centered throughout our search. To "follow our bliss" can be one of the greatest challenges of our lives. It requires times of soul searching, humility, and trust in the unknown. The I Ching suggests that only by plumbing our own depths are we able to find the answers to our career questions and emerge buoyant and ready to focus our energies on our new work goals.

Enhance your Career area when:

- you are making any kind of change in your job or career;
- you are looking for or changing your job or career;
- you want to volunteer or do community service work; or
- you are going from one type of work into another.

The Career Bagua in Action

EVE'S GARDEN

Eve had to admit that her career was not going well. Even though her life was satisfying in every other way, her job was stressing her out. Six years ago, her results as a marketing agent had been remarkable. But, gradually and steadily, her effectiveness had gone downhill. At first, she blamed it on her boss, but when he was replaced, the slow decline continued. She knew she was good at what she did, so what could it be? On the advice of a friend, she decided to make a Feng Shui appointment.

Eve lived on the right side of a duplex. As I walked up to her side of the house, I noticed the landscaping was in great need of loving care, and her front door's screen was rusted to a bright orange. Her front entrance was exactly in the Career area of her side of the building and was surrounded by a haggard outline of what used to be a flower garden. A few weeds struggled to survive in the parched ground, and the soil around the cement stairs leading to Eve's door was washed away, exposing dark cracks and anthills. There was nothing lively or attractive about her front entrance, and I wondered before I knocked on the door if she was having career problems.

Eve ushered me into her home. Once inside, beauty surrounded me. Her home was absolutely lovely, appointed with things she loved, including a wonderful ceramics collection. I knew our work would not take place inside, but outside.

Treatments and Results:

It was no surprise to discover that Eve was not a gardener. She was reluctant to even talk about the outside area until I pointed out its importance to her career. She looked around wide-eyed at the weeds and bare dirt. "I can't believe this yard has anything do to with my career!" she exclaimed. I suggested that she do some simple enhancements and just see what happened. First, she was to put two big pots of red flowers such as geraniums on either side of the steps leading to her front door. They would be her "greeters" and would help to adjust the deteriorating Ch'i.

Next, I suggested that she pull the weeds out of the old flower bed and plant very easy-to-care-for flowers there, then add a birdbath to bring in the water element, attract wildlife, and enliven the Ch'i. Third, I suggested that she mulch around the stairs, to cover the cracks and give the soil a chance to regenerate. Fourth, restore her "mouth of Ch'i" by removing the rust from her front door screen and painting it the Career color of black. And fifth, hang a wind chime or whirlygig of her choice near the front door to call in the positive Ch'i. She agreed to do these things, in the spirit of enhancing her career. Inside, I pointed out the Career area in each room, and made sure that she understood that the things located there were acting as environmental affirmations for her career goals as well.

Two weeks later, Eve called me. She sounded very excited on the phone. She just had to tell me what had happened! She had dutifully done all the things I'd suggested outside. She'd even added a hummingbird feeder. And, boy, had things begun to change at work—radically. Two prospects she had been working on for over a year suddenly signed up for her company's services. She could hardly believe it. But that wasn't the best news.

"I've just signed up the biggest client of my whole career, and he came to *me*! I tell you," she said, "I don't even care about my nails anymore—I'm digging in my garden every chance I get, and it already looks like a little paradise.

I've decided I'm going to plant a flower in honor of each new client I sign up."

That was two years ago, and Eve's career is going stronger than ever. When her colleagues ask her what her secret is, she starts off her explanation by inquiring: "Have you ever heard of Feng Shui?..."

▼▼▼

DONNA'S DOOR

This is one of my favorite stories because it shows how powerful the Bagua can be, whether people know they're working with it or not.

Donna received the gift of a Feng Shui appointment from her mother, who wanted her daughter to experience a consultation. When Donna called to make her appointment, I asked if she really wanted to receive this gift. She answered with an enthusiastic YES!

Her home was in a neighborhood that I had never visited before. I drove slowly down her street, taking in the surroundings. It was an older neighborhood, with the condition of the homes ranging from excellent to poor. One home stood out from all the rest. Both the house and the landscaping were picture-perfect, very inviting, showing exceptional attention to detail. It turned out to be Donna's home.

I parked and stood in front of her house for a few minutes. I could see that she had added a large front deck that led to a new front door and enclosed foyer. The addition had greatly enhanced the Bagua of the house, with the elegant new front door located in the Career area. Although the addition didn't stretch across the whole front of the house, leaving Knowledge and Self-Cultivation outside, Donna had landscaped the area with a variety of flowers and a large tree planted precisely in the "missing" corner. I was impressed!

The first question I asked Donna was, "Have you had any career changes lately?"

"Did my mom tell you?" she asked. "I've just been awarded a fabulous promotion, and I will be doing what I've always wanted to do. I've been working toward this for years. There was so much competition; I'm still blown away that I was the one to receive it."

"Tell me, when did you build on this new entrance?" I asked.

"Well, let's see, it was about a three-month project that was completed about a month ago. I remember because I was jumping through all those hoops to get my promotion about the same time. Why?"

I laughed, thinking about how perfect her story was. I explained to her how, according to Feng Shui, she had greatly enhanced her career Ch'i by changing the front entrance the way she did. As I talked, she kept saying, "I didn't know...that's amazing...I didn't have a clue!"

We talked about how to arrange Donna's new foyer area so that it remained open and free of clutter. Instead of being greeted by a crowded coat-tree as we entered, I suggested that she place a glass-topped table with a dark base (symbolizing the Water element) associated with Career, and a chair or two there to give the foyer a warm, welcoming feeling. The new arrangement would also open up the lovely view to the living room through the original exterior windows, now a part of the foyer. There was plenty of room for the coat-tree behind the door, where it would be convenient, yet out of view when first entering the house.

"Keeping the threshold of your front door clean and clear lets your guests know how much you honor and appreciate them. And, in this case, it will continually enhance your career Ch'i," I said. "You'll take on your new promotion with a clear and open mind, an expansive viewpoint, and the energy to graciously welcome all the new opportunities coming your way."

Personalized Enhancements for Career

Choose one or a combination of things on the following list to personally enhance your Career areas:

- Water features such as fountains, waterfalls, and aquariums
- Posters, paintings, collages, photos; and art depicting streams, oceans, lakes, waterfalls, ponds, etc.
- Career images and symbols
- Items in black, and very dark colors such as navy blue, deep maroon, chocolate brown, and charcoal gray
- Randomly shaped and free-form items
- Mirrors, glass, and crystal items
- Quotes, affirmations, and sayings relating to Career
- Other things that have a personal association to Career

Affirmations for Career

Choose any of the following affirmations that strike a chord of truth in you, write them down, and put them in the Career area of your home, workplace, office, desk, or any other Career area you are working with. Or, use them as a guide in writing your own personal Career affirmations.

My career is fulfilling, inspiring, and lucrative.

I grow and prosper through performing my life's work.

I express my life's purpose through my career.

I express my creativity, my joy, and my enthusiasm in my work.

I attract many positive opportunities and circumstances.

I am open to knowing and living my true calling.

The Bagua Map
KNOWLEDGE AND SELF-CULTIVATION

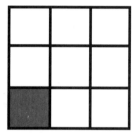

Your Knowledge and Self-Cultivation area is located in the front left section of the structure you are working with. (See the Bagua Map on page 62.)

The I Ching's Wisdom on Knowledge and Self-Cultivation

The I Ching trigram, *Ken*, meaning "Mountain," is associated with Knowledge and Self-Cultivation. This teaching states that there is a direct link between a calm mind and an intelligent mind. It is a courageous act to focus the mind on newly acquired knowledge. However, we assimilate our knowledge best when we also cultivate a peaceful mind by practicing some form of regular "keeping still," such as meditation, contemplation, and introspection. The mountain symbolizes taking the time to climb to the quiet heights within ourselves, to contemplate our experiences, and to return, having integrated them. This is the act of cultivating ourselves. Becoming truly knowledgeable is far more complex than simply gathering information. Knowledge is viewed as the seed of wisdom. It grows through the nourishing influences of both study and contemplation. The I Ching reminds us that when we spend time on the mountain, our fields of knowledge will be lush and productive.

Enhance your Knowledge and Self-Cultivation areas when:

- you are a student of any subject at any time;
- you are in counseling or any kind of self-growth activity; or
- you want to cultivate a more peaceful mind or lifestyle.

Knowledge and Self-Cultivation Bagua in Action

HAVE IT HER WAY

Christine and her daughter Angie lived in a magnificent home overlooking the ocean. They had everything money could buy. So why was Angie suffering from insomnia? And why had she become such a poor student in the last few months? She'd always been a smart, well-adjusted teenager before. Now she was listless and pale, shying away from participating in the same kind of school projects she had always loved. Christine, being an observant and concerned mother, had determined it wasn't drugs or diet. The family doctor called it a phase. Christine wasn't convinced. She decided to have a Feng Shui consultation.

Christine took me through their sunny home. I asked her if Angie had given me permission to look at her room—a very important part of practicing Feng Shui. Christine assured me that she had.

Angie's room was definitely decorated in "teenager." She had recently painted the walls in a dark, intense green, which made me feel like I was standing in deep woods on a dark night. She had also rearranged all of her furniture. I made note that the door into the room was located on the left in the Knowledge and Self-Cultivation area. A hamper of dirty clothes stood behind the door so that the door could only open halfway. I asked Christine if the environment change correlated with the insomnia and poor study habits. She paused as she thought back, and realized it was shortly after Angie had changed everything that her whole mood had soured. And, it had gotten worse as time passed.

Suddenly, Christine was ready to tear the room apart, paint it white, and put all the furniture back where it had been before. "I can't believe changing a room could change a person so much!" she exclaimed.

I suggested that we relax and take a detailed look around the room. My attention was drawn to the punk rock posters that were hanging in the Health area directly across from the bed. The skeletons and bloody knives were certainly scary enough to keep me awake. Also, the dark green walls were becoming more oppressive by the minute, and kept any light from really brightening the room.

Angie's desk had been moved to the back of the room with the chair facing away from the door. The top was piled with magazines, jewelry, belts, and scarves, leaving no room for studying.

"When she first rearranged everything, her desk was perfect. But, that didn't last long," said Christine.

Treatments and Results:

"The changes I'm going to suggest need to be agreed to by your daughter," I said, "or they probably won't work."

"She's so unhappy now," bemoaned Christine. "I think she'll be very receptive to your ideas."

I began by suggesting that Angie's hamper be moved into one of the large closets in the room so that the door could fully open. "This will make her feel completely open to the positive opportunities in her life," I explained.

Next, the dark green walls needed to change. I suggested that she wallpaper over the paint with a pastel paper. Let Angie pick it out, but guide her toward neutral pastels without much of a pattern. She could possibly leave the green paint below a pastel chair rail, and paper above. "The green is too dark over too much surface area, and will make anyone living with it feel heavy and depressed," I said.

Third, we needed to address the posters. Here we had art depicting graphic violence that Angie thought she liked. I suggested two possibilities: ideally, she would take the posters down and choose new art that was soothing and inspirational. If she insisted on keeping them up, the second choice would be to move the bed away from them so that she couldn't see them before going to sleep. Christine began to conjure up a plan to take Angie shopping for art. I asked her to please keep in mind that if Angie was not ready to change the posters, she would probably choose new art in the same theme. "Better to let her tell you when she's ready," I said.

Fourth, the desk needed to be moved up close to the door at the front of the room into the Knowledge and Self-Cultivation area. Placed there, the desk would be the first thing Angie saw when she came into the room, and she could see the door when sitting at it. A bright desk lamp was also essential and needed to be kept on all the time to attract and strengthen the Ch'i until Angie was back on track.

The paraphernalia on the desk led me to the closets, which were completely chaotic. We talked about having the closets fitted with organizers that really worked for Angie, with plenty of drawers and hooks for her expressive wardrobe.

I didn't talk to Christine again for several months. One day I bumped into her and asked how she and Angie were.

"Oh, we're just great," she said. "You know, all kinds of good things have happened since our appointment." She described the sequence of events over the last few months. Angie had been overwhelmed by all the suggestions. At first, she was only willing to move her hamper and her desk. It seemed to Christine that as soon as her desk was near the door, she began to use it for schoolwork. Then she noticed that Angie had moved her bed away from her posters, and was sleeping much better.

"She kept her room like that for about two months, and I thought she had done enough, because she had more energy, and was participating in her school play." Christina said. "Then, she came to me one day and said she wanted to sponge the dark green walls with white paint, like one of her friends had done."

Apparently, Angie and her friend spent the better part of a weekend sponging her room, and the effect was dazzling.

"After that weekend, Angie was truly herself again," Christina remembered. "She became the live wire I had always known her to be. I think she's going to be an actress!"

"What happened to the posters?" I asked.

"Well," Christina said, "they had to come down for the paint job, and Angie hasn't put them back up. She's into angels now, and they're all over her room."

▼▼▼

RUNNING ON EMPTY

Jenny wanted some Feng Shui advice on her plans for home improvement. She would come home after long days of work and night school and fantasize about how to improve her house. Since most of her plans involved tearing down walls and enlarging rooms, she decided that it was time for some professional feedback. I could tell from our telephone conversation that Jenny was a whirlwind of energy since I wasn't able to complete a single sentence during our phone conversation. Her mental processes struck me as frenzied and chaotic. My interest in her house was piqued.

Jenny's home was a rectangular shape, with the front entrance in the Career area and the garage in the Knowledge and Self-Cultivation area. She flew out of her door to greet me and rushed me through the house on a general tour. As we went, she explained her long line of fantasies and ideas about how to make the house bigger, better, sunnier, and more beautiful. We came to a sudden halt in front of the interior garage door. Jenny turned to guide me back into the living room, saying that the garage was off-limits.

"But it's part of the house, Jenny, and in Feng Shui, every part counts," I explained.

"Well, as far as I'm concerned, it doesn't," she countered.

I suggested that we sit down and talk about Feng Shui principles and the Bagua Map. If she still didn't want me to see the garage after that, it was fine. I could tell that she wasn't happy about this, but I had a strong feeling the garage was the main problem. I explained that the Ch'i in the garage was interrelated with the rest of the house, and that it held the Ch'i of Knowledge and Self-Cultivation for her. This was an especially important area to check out due to her current enrollment in night school. She was uncharacteristically quiet as she processed this unforeseen bit of knowledge. All she had really expected from her Feng Shui appointment was to find out which walls to move!

"The things you have in your garage are talking to you all the time," I said. "Just be sure they're saying nice things."

Jenny groaned. "Well, I'm not sure we'll be able to hear ourselves think in there, but you might as well see it."

The garage was in complete and utter chaos. It was a collage of furniture and other things piled and hung at different angles from floor to ceiling. She had managed to keep an area carved out for her car, with the path between it and the door into the house barely discernible.

"What can I say? I keep thinking I'll be able to use this stuff or sell it or give it to friends," Jenny explained. "Are you telling me that all this junk affects my ability to think?"

"To think clearly, yes," I said. "Every time you drive in here, and every time you even think about the garage, it probably boggles your mind."

"Gosh, maybe this is why I feel so jangled all the time," she mused. "I always feel overwhelmed with what needs to be done. My mind is never still."

"And you want to do more with this house...." I said. "Let me suggest that you make this garage your first project. Clean it, organize it, and your whole life will probably change. Here's your Feng Shui assignment: Have a huge garage sale, organize your garage in general, and learn some kind of meditation or introspection technique. My prediction is that your mental clarity and calmness will dramatically improve."

Treatments and Results:

Our appointment plunged Jenny into some deep soul searching. Why was she hanging on to all those things in her garage? Was she really pursuing the right course of study? Why was she so frantic all the time anyway? She realized that deep down inside, she was completely exhausted and needed to take some time for herself. She had three garage sales to pare down her junk collection and made a nice chunk of cash in the process. She used the extra money to learn meditation techniques and get a much-needed rest at a mountain retreat center. By the time she came back, she had decided to continue her studies, but to slow them down to one night a week to give herself more "down" time.

During our most recent conversation, I noticed that I was able to finish all of my sentences, and that Jenny was calm and relaxed.

"What about your plans to enlarge the house?" I asked.

"Oh, forget it," she answered. "I realize I have plenty of space for everything. I can't quite believe that cleaning out that horrible mess in the garage could somehow be connected to my enjoying my life more, but it looks to me like that's exactly what happened."

Personalized Enhancements for Knowledge and Self-Cultivation:

Choose one or more things from the following list to personally enhance your Knowledge and Self-Cultivation Bagua area:

- Books, tapes, and other material currently being studied
- Posters, paintings, collages, and photos of mountains and quiet places; and figures of teachers and wise people in your life in meditation, contemplation, or repose
- Things in the colors of black, blue, and green
- Quotes, affirmations, and inspirational sayings pertaining to

Knowledge and Self-Cultivation
- Other things that have a personal association to Knowledge and Self-Cultivation

Affirmations for Knowledge and Self-Cultivation

Choose any of the affirmations listed below that you resonate with, write them down, and place them in the Knowledge and Self-Cultivation area of your home, office, desk, or any other place you are working with. You can also use the ones listed below as a guide in writing your own personal affirmations.

I easily and joyfully assimilate new knowledge and information.

I trust my learning process.

Knowing that I am constantly learning and growing, I relax into each moment of my life.

I am peaceful and calm as I share my knowledge with others.

I am a wise and knowledgeable person.

In all situations, I always know what to do and say.

▼▼▼

THE CENTER OF THE BAGUA MAP

The Center of the Bagua Map is considered the neutral area, a perfect balance of yin and yang, a place of peace. There is no trigram, and no one single facet of life associated with it. Life flows and circles around the Center. It is a perfect area to place a meditation, contemplation, or "quiet" room, an atrium, or some object or piece of art that reminds you to stay centered throughout all your activities. The Center of the Bagua is related to the element of Earth, suggesting the importance of arranging our lives to flow around a solid base. The Center is strengthened when we create personal paradises to live and work in, and when we cultivate a sense of being grounded and centered within ourselves.

The Earth element is related to the color yellow, as well as all earth-tones. It is also symbolized by the shape of the square or rectangle. Think of a Chinese coin, and you will see the square "Earth" shape cut out of the middle of the round coin.

▼▼▼ ▼▼▼

I am drawn to beauty as a tree
is drawn to light or an animal to
water. It is nourishment and a
reality that does not ignore
those qualities that are
considered ugly but touches on
truth in the nature of things.

—*Andy Goldsworthy*

BASIC FENG SHUI TOOLS FOR ENHANCING CH'I

There are basic Feng Shui tools that are time-proven remedies for treating, stabilizing, enhancing, and balancing the Ch'i in an environment. You can select items from this list to enhance your home and workplace in general, as well as when you're working with the Bagua Map.

To receive the greatest benefit from your enhancements, be sure that you genuinely like your selections. Make them yours. There are countless combinations you can put together to create positive, pleasing results. Let your creativity and style really shine through while practicing Feng Shui. Your enhancements will always work best when you personally delight in them every time you see them.

The ten basic tools are:

1) *Colors*

Colors perpetually surround us and have a powerful impact on us.

We are conditioned by the many cultural, seasonal, and symbolic meanings and associations that colors have. For instance, white is the color associated with weddings and purity in America. In China, white is often associated with grieving and death. Red is the color often used to alert us to danger in America, while in China, it is the color of celebration and good fortune. Black is our color of mourning and death, while in China, black is associated with the abundant flow of wealth and auspicious circumstances.

In Feng Shui, colors are primarily used to represent the five elements and the nine areas in the Bagua Map. Surrounding ourselves with a variety of colors balances the overall Ch'i in our environments. We can stimulate positive change and vitality by purposefully applying colors as specific enhancements to our homes and offices. When you work with color as a Feng Shui tool, always choose tones you love. The color red can range from pink to burgundy; blue, from teal to navy, and so on. Work with color as you would any other Bagua enhancement—as a powerful tool for creating your personal paradise. And, as always, if the Specific Bagua colors don't appeal to you, choose another way to enhance the Bagua or balance the Elements.

The color associations are given in plurals because, as mentioned above, every color has myriad variations. (See the chart on the next page.)

Colors in your Bagua areas can be applied in a wide variety of ways. A wall in the Wealth area may be painted with a vivid or pastel shade of lavender, blue, or red. Art pieces of all kinds may be chosen for their color, such as a scroll of black calligraphed characters in the Career area, a blue and green landscape in the Health and Family area, or a pink alabaster sculpture of lovers in the Love and Marriage area. Furnishings and upholstery can be colorful Bagua additions, such as a green bookshelf in the Knowledge area, a burgundy leather reading chair in the Fame area, or a bright white table in the Children and Creativity area.

Color can be subtly or vividly used to balance and enhance the five elements. You may choose to work with the elements strictly through the use of color. An aqua carpet (Wood) with mauve or peach walls (Fire) and a ceiling in an earthtone such as taupe or beige (Earth), with creamy white furniture (Metal) and black or dark accessories (Water) is an example of all the elements being represented strictly through color in one room.

All the basic colors may also be captured in one dramatic piece. You can transform a very neutral room by adding one well-chosen piece that colorfully represents all the elements.

BAGUA AREA	ELEMENT	COLORS
Health & Family	Wood	Blues and greens
Wealth & Prosperity		Blues, reds, and purples
Fame & Reputation	Fire	Reds
Love & Marriage		Reds, pinks, and white
Creativity & Children	Metal	White and pastels
Helpful People & Travel		White, grays, and blacks
Career	Water	Black and darktones
Knowledge & Self-Cultivation		Black, blues, and greens
Center	Earth	Yellows and earthtones

2) *Mirrors*

Mirrors activate, enhance, and circulate Ch'i. In Feng Shui, they correct many problems by enlarging rooms, amplifying existing light, providing protection, rerouting Ch'i, bringing out "disappearing" walls, and doubling existing windows and views. Popularly known as the "aspirin of Feng Shui," mirrors are relied on for opening up small spaces and restoring balance to claustrophobic or architecturally lop-sided areas. They are often used in foyers to give people a grander feeling as they are entering the building. When two walls in the same room are different heights, a mirror can be installed on the shorter wall to lift the Ch'i and balance out the appearance of the architecture. When corners protrude into a room, or stairways come careening down from an upper level, mirrors are situated in such a way as to reflect these structural culprits and circulate the Ch'i back around again.

The general rule of thumb in mirror size is "the bigger, the better." Mirroring a whole wall often creates a dynamic, positive change in a room, while enhancing one or more Bagua areas. Whether large or small, all mirrors should be hung so that at least your entire head is reflected. It can deplete your Ch'i to see your image cut off and have to lower or raise yourself from a natural standing position to see your image. Mirrors that distort or chop up images should be avoided, such as mirror tiles, fancy overlapped beveled models, or foggy antique mirrors.

Elementally, mirrors are related to Water. Since Water controls Fire, mirrors are often placed over fireplaces to balance the fiery Ch'i with reflective Water.

Mirrors can be used to introduce the shapes that correlate with any of the elements and Bagua areas. For instance, a circular or oval mirror, the shape of the Metal element, can be used when enhancing the Creativity and Children area. You can also frame a mirror in the color or material associated with the Bagua. The long columnlike shape of a wardrobe mirror, framed in wood, is a perfect enhancement for the Health and Family area. Mirrors can also establish a comforting sense of safety in any room. Placed so that they reflect the entrance, mirrors report activity to people sitting with their backs to the door.

There are several places where mirrors are not advisable. Mirrors hung at the end of a long hallway only double its length. Instead, hang mirrors on walls across from the doors that open onto the hall. This widens the hall and adjusts people's Ch'i as they enter the hall from a doorway. Mirrors that face a bed can be unnerving, especially to people who get up during the night. Reflected movements can frighten a half-asleep person and should be avoided.

Remember: mirrors stimulate and circulate Ch'i, and can bring too much "awake" energy into a bedroom. And, no matter how big and beautiful, mirrors hung across from each other create images that seem to go on into infinity, disorienting people and depleting vital Ch'i.

3) *Lighting*

Lighting includes electrical (incandescent and halogen) oil, candles, and natural sunlight. Lighting is often a quick and easy way to bring additional Ch'i into an area with its warmth and illumination, especially areas that are dark to begin with. Lights are also used to symbolically lift a low ceiling, especially lighting that points up.

Outdoors, lights such as lampposts or uplighting can be used to anchor a missing Bagua area. People with properties that are located at the bottom of a hill, or in a low-lying area, can install lighting on the four corners of the house to symbolically lift the location.

As with other basic Feng Shui enhancements, light fixtures can be chosen to represent the colors or element associated with a Bagua area, such as a red lamp in the Fame and Reputation area, or green and blue candles in the Health and Family area.

The typical fluorescent bulbs emit only part of the light spectrum, depleting the Ch'i of a room and of the people working or living there. Fluorescent light fixtures can be fitted with full-spectrum bulbs that begin to solve the problem. However, fluorescent bulbs flicker, depleting people's Ch'i. Incandescent and halogen lighting, used in one or more of the Bagua areas, even in a fluorescent-lit room, serves a dual purpose—it enhances the Bagua area, and helps balance the lighting in general. Whenever possible, reduce or eliminate fluorescent lighting that is directly overhead for long periods of time.

Fireplaces can be a wonderful source of heat and light, and are powerful representations of the Fire element. However, because they are often large in size, they can be too fiery, and actually "burn" up the Ch'i in the area where they are located. To balance a fireplace, you can:

- Always keep the fireplace arranged with logs to give the impression of fire and provide an aesthetic point of focus.
- Elementally balance Fire by placing a symbol of Water near the fireplace. Examples of Water symbols include a bowl of water, an interior water feature, a mirror, glass fireplace doors, or crystal ornamentation.
- Place healthy plants, fresh flowers, or an artful screen in front of the fireplace opening when not in use.
- Be creative and fashion your own "grotto" in the fireplace opening, using candles, specimen rocks, potpourri, water bowls, statues, incense, etc.

4) Crystals

Round faceted crystals are used in Feng Shui to balance Ch'i that's moving too fast or too slow for human comfort. They disperse raging Ch'i and activate sluggish Ch'i. As regulators, they can draw in and circulate Ch'i from a small window, or break up and circulate the speeding Ch'i cascading down a stairwell or hallway. Because of their compact size, they are often used where there's no room for another cure to be placed, such as in a narrow hallway or tiny foyer. Hung well overhead, they do their job of circulating Ch'i unobtrusively, which can be a benefit in a Western household or office. But, despite their size, crystals are powerful Ch'i directors and can be used as a constant enhancement in any Bagua area, or to balance structural flaws.

The shape of the classic Feng Shui cut-glass crystal is round, to fully circulate the Ch'i in an area. The size of the crystal depends upon the size of the area it's going to hang in. You don't want it to be too big, though, or it can seem threatening overhead. In most cases, a round faceted crystal the size of a quarter to a 50-cent piece will do the trick.

Other shapes, such as faceted octagons, hearts, and raindrops, are wonderful Ch'i enhancers when placed near windows to catch the sun and fill the area with rainbows. Rainbows tend to inspire and uplift people's Ch'i, and are a great way to bring in all the elemental colors.

Cut-glass crystals are specifically associated with the Water element and can be used to bring balance to areas dominated by the Fire element, such as in a very sunny window.

5) *Sound Makers*

Harmonious sound makers, such as wind chimes, wind sculptures, bells, and musical instruments "call in" benevolent Ch'i. They summon new opportunities with their appealing sounds when placed in any Bagua area, such as in Career, Love, and Creativity areas.

It's important that the sounds made by these objects be completely melodious to your ears. For instance, wind chimes can sound either heavenly or discordant, so pick those that lift your spirits with their sound.

Musical instruments can also be strategically placed in a Bagua area that needs attuned Ch'i. Bamboo flutes are a classic Bagua enhancement, hung to uplift and direct Ch'i.

Music that is chosen for its mellifluous quality is a powerful way to uplift the Ch'i in any environment. Stressful office and home environments can be soothed and calmed by the right music or recorded nature sounds such as those evoking the ocean, a meadow, or a forest. Music also adds positive Ch'i to any of your Bagua areas. Determine which type of music elicits romantic, creative, or directive thoughts and feelings in you, and use it to enhance the Bagua areas you are working with.

6) *Living Things*

This category includes all things that require regular maintenance, such as plants, flowers, pets, and wildlife.

Healthy plants and fresh flowers are potent carriers of positive Ch'i. In Feng Shui, they can be used in any of the Bagua areas with great success. Flowering plants and cut flowers can be chosen to correlate with the Bagua colors, as well as the vases and pots they're placed in. For instance, a violet gloxinia plant in a blue ceramic pot can enliven the Wealth area, red carnations in a red glass vase can enhance the Fame area, while a pure white cyclamen plant in a white basket can uplift the Creativity and Children area.

When choosing plants, look for those that have wide, rounded, "friendly" leaves, such as jade and pothos, or a generally soft, graceful appearance, such as ficus, and most palms. Plants with threateningly sharp or pointed leaves are not recommended for enhancing Bagua areas. Plants in this category include yucca and sago palm. You'll recognize them immediately; they are the ones that "bite" when you touch their tips. Be sure to match the lighting requirements of any plant with the light that is available in a location. In general, cacti with stickers are not recommended unless you have a positive personal association with them that relates to a Bagua area.

Silk and plastic plants and flowers can be used to replace living plant material. Artificial plants and flowers are sometimes the best choice when lighting is too low or maintenance is a problem. Whether alive or not, the important thing is that they appear healthy and lush. Unhealthy or unkempt plants only deaden the Ch'i wherever they are located. Make sure you keep your Bagua plants and flowers happy and healthy. This means changing out cut flowers as soon as they show signs of dying, and potted plants when they are sickly, straggly, or insect-infested. Using any Bagua area as a plant hospital is NOT recommended!

Outside, trees and gardens can balance the Bagua when located in areas that need enhancement. For instance, a beautiful tree can be planted to be the "corner" that squares off and completes an L-shaped building. Landscaping around the tree brings more revitalizing Ch'i to the area. Flowers and plants can be chosen to represent the specific colors and shapes related to the Bagua area you are working with, such as pink roses in the Love area, or red impatiens in the Wealth area. Your Bagua Garden can be a canvas of sorts, where you "paint with plants," creating a unique and dynamic masterpiece that feeds you with beauty and energy every time you see it.

Plants and flowers are symbols of the Wood element, and can be used when balancing an environment that is dominated by the Earth element—such as a home that's square, with square and rectangular windows, doors, and furniture. Many of our Western buildings fit this description.

Pets, like plants and people, need tender loving care, and will reward you for it with their vitality and personality. Even elderly pets, when loved and cared for, continue to enhance the Ch'i throughout their golden years. However, a pet that is not well cared for will deplete the Ch'i in its environment dramatically. Be sure all pets are having their needs met, including the children's hamster, the company fish, and the new kittens. We can call more vital Ch'i in by feeding the wild birds and other forms of wildlife when appropriate. A wildlife sanctuary can be a wonderful choice for enhancing an outdoor Bagua area. A simple birdfeeder in an urban window can bring Nature with all its nourishing Ch'i close enough to be enjoyed every day.

Whether they are wild or tame, animals are associated with the Fire element.

7) *Objects of Nature*

Objects of Nature are those things that don't require active maintenance and care, such as rocks, pine cones, dried flowers, driftwood, shells, potpourri, and incense. When endowed with personal meaning, these objects can be powerful enhancers of the Ch'i in your home or office. A beautiful shell found during a honeymoon is a perfect piece for a Bagua area related to Love and Marriage. Seed pods picked during a business retreat can symbolize a blossoming career. Specimen rocks in all the colors of the rainbow are reminders of artistic expression in the Bagua area related to Creativity.

Objects of Nature such as rocks, boulders, and logs may be incorporated into an outdoor Bagua arrangement. Chosen for their shape, size, and markings, rocks and boulders are often seen as precious art forms in China, and can be as expensive as intricately carved statues. They are considered great storers of natural energy and give a strong dose of good Ch'i to the Bagua area where they're located. When logs, driftwood, and branches take on beautiful sculptural shapes, they inspire our imaginations while enhancing the Ch'i. They can be placed as either primary or accent garden pieces in any Bagua area. All objects of Nature have many faces. When working with them, position them so that their inspirational qualities are highlighted, like a jewel in a setting.

8) Water Features

Interior and exterior water features move and stimulate Ch'i. Fountains and waterfalls have both a visual and an auditory component as they circulate and refresh the Ch'i, while providing a pleasing place to rest the eye and the ear.

Be sure to adjust the sound until it's "just right" to your ear, because, whether they are indoors or outdoors, fountains adjusted incorrectly can increase your visits to the bathroom.

Interior fountains and waterfalls are excellent choices for enhancing the Ch'i in any Bagua area in your home or workplace. They are considered especially powerful in the Wealth and Career areas, because the element of water has a direct association with the flow of money. A fountain or waterfall can become the centerpiece for an enchanting indoor sanctuary when complemented with plants, rocks, and other nature objects.

Water features are also excellent choices for balancing "missing" exterior Bagua areas and enhancing the Ch'i outside your home or office. Placed to "fill in" where the corner or outside wall of the building would be, they symbolically complete the structure, while assuring the constant flow and circulation of lively Ch'i. To balance structure, exterior water features need to be significant in size, and faced toward the building, if applicable. The larger the building, the bigger they need to be to balance the missing area. For instance, a home that's about 2,000 square feet needs a water feature at least four feet tall.

Any exterior water feature will attract wildlife, awakening and enlivening the Ch'i even further. Urns, bowls, pools, and birdbaths filled with clean water are all Ch'i-enhancing options when their size is appropriate for the location.

9) Wind Dancers

Whether brightly colored and whimsical, or serious art pieces, "wind dancers" such as mobiles, whirligigs, banners, flags, and weathervanes uplift and invigorate the Ch'i.

Inside, they are often used to fill in open space provided by large rooms and high ceilings. For example, a rich royal purple banner hung from a high ceiling in the Wealth area adds a three-dimensional point of interest, as well as a constant reminder of prosperity and abundance. Mobiles range widely in size, and can be made of anything, including crystals, nature objects, metal, paper, and glass. A crystal mobile hung in the Creativity area symbolically generates new ideas and inspiration. A nature mobile in the Health area is a reminder of the deep sense of well-being Nature brings to us. A mobile of artwork depicting angels poised in the Helpful People area reminds us of the blessings and synchronicities people bring into our lives.

Outdoors, wind dancers call in and circulate the Ch'i with their movements and visual appeal. They attract attention and good Ch'i to businesses and homes alike and can make memorable landmarks. A flagpole can be used to mark a building's missing corner, symbolically completing the building's shape. The displayed flag should represent something you love—your country, your colors, your special interest, your symbol or logo. Whirligigs and banners hung from decks, porches, and eaves lift the Ch'i and enhance the Bagua areas of a building.

10) Art

Art of all kinds, including paintings, sculptures, collages, and textiles, have a powerful effect on people. The general rule of thumb is that to secure the Ch'i in various Bagua areas, and to enhance the Ch'i in general, art needs to elicit the positive images and feelings that relate to the area being enhanced. For instance, romantic art is best when placed in the Love area; art pieces that are powerful and dynamic belong in the Career, Wealth, and Fame areas; soothing works of art enhance the Bagua area related to Health; inspirational art goes well in the Knowledge and Self-Cultivation and Helpful People and Travel areas; whimsical, brightly colored art uplifts the Creativity and Children area.

When choosing art to enhance a Bagua area, look for pieces that really "speak" to you. If the art is for a room in the house that's shared by other people, be sure they like it, too. Ideally, the art will depict wholesome images and pleasing colors, and will give you a positive lift every time you see it. Violent, gruesome, or unhappy subjects are not considered good choices for enhancing the Bagua. Pay special attention to the art you currently have in the Bagua areas you want to enhance. If you find that it does not accurately and beautifully reflect your goals and wishes, replace it with art that does.

In one case, a couple discovered that they had hung a painting of a sad-looking woman sitting alone at a table in their Love area. Their main complaint was that the wife felt as if she spent too much time alone waiting for her husband to return from work. Remember: it is better to have no art than art that doesn't make your heart sing.

Outdoors, art and sculptures ground and stabilize Ch'i with their weight and presence. Obviously, the larger they are, the more powerful they can be in symbolically balancing the Ch'i around the outside of a building. Depending on their size and location, outdoor art and sculptures offer a potent message to the people who see them. A great example is the Statue of Liberty standing at the entrance to New York Harbor and welcoming people to a new life.

Consider making your own art. You can collect images of your ideal partner, career, family, health, or wealth, and make them into a collage. When you do this, you are literally gathering the Ch'i to enhance your life. Draw, paint, weave, build, or sculpt images that symbolize your ideals. What color is your reputation? What shape is your knowledge? What image is your career? When you create your own art, you are striking a very personal chord to achieve a specific result. Your Ch'i literally forms your art piece for the purpose of enhancing your life. Powerful results often come out of this process.

The spiritual symbols that are personally meaningful to you are potent, attracting, uplifting and revitalizing the Ch'i surrounding their location. Spiritual or religious symbols include images of angels, saints, great teachers, gods, goddesses, and mystics. Books such as the Bible, the Koran, and the Upanishads are also considered spiritual symbols; as well as distinct shapes such as the cross, the pointed star, or the sri yantra. Here again, the key is that these symbols have personal inspirational meaning for you. Place them in any Bagua area where you really feel you need help. The Helpful People area and Knowledge and Self-Cultivation area are often directly related to spiritual development and assistance, and can be symbolized by a tiny angel, religious figure, or a whole altar that includes many meaningful items.

Hold every moment sacred. Give each clarity and meaning, each the weight of your awareness.

—*Thomas Mann*

9

BAGUA
BLESSINGS

Throughout the course of our lives, we give and receive blessings in many celebratory forms, such as baptisms, christenings, confirmations, bar mitzvahs, weddings, and birthdays. When we view our habitats as being as alive, dynamic, and animated as we are, it makes sense to honor them from time to time with a special blessing. Blessings you may already be familiar with include housewarming parties, sage burning, and cutting the ribbon ceremoniously tied across a new threshold.

The Bagua Map is the template we will use for Indoor and Outdoor Bagua Blessings. Bagua blessings are performed inside or outside a building to protect and seal in the good wishes and positive Ch'i of the people who live or work there. They are appropriate anytime you want to balance and strengthen the Ch'i of a home or workplace. A Bagua Blessing is a wonderful way to empower people to realize their innermost hopes, dreams, and goals. In the case of a couple, they have an opportunity to contemplate and focus on their own individual aspirations, voice them, and listen to their partner's. They hear each others' hopes and prayers, and are inevitably touched by what they may never have heard before. A Bagua Blessing can take place in an office, where each participant discovers how unique, complementary, or surprising their colleagues' desires and wishes are. In addition to blessing the building itself, Bagua Blessings are almost always deepening, heart-opening experiences that build and strengthen the positive Ch'i between people.

Indoor Bagua Blessings

Indoor Bagua Blessings may be done alone, with the other people who live or work in the home or office, or with a group gathered specif-ically to participate in the Blessing. You will need nine candles, and appropriate dishes or candlesticks to hold them. Decide on what kind of candles you'd like to use, such as votives in the various Bagua colors, tapers, or white tealight candles. Before you begin your Blessing, you can place one candle in each of the Bagua areas, and one in the center area of the building. Or, you can carry them with you throughout the Blessing, placing one in each area as you go.

You begin your Bagua Blessing by standing or sitting in the Bagua area associated with Health and Family. Enter into a receptive, medita-tive state of mind. Light your candle and pause for a moment of reflec-tion on what hopes, aspirations, goals, and wishes you have concerning your health and family. When you are ready, say them aloud, even if you are alone. Take your time. When other people are present who live or work there, they also take a turn speaking their hopes, dreams, and good wishes that relate to their health and family. Then, invite anyone participating who doesn't live or work there to verbally extend their blessings to the health and family of the people who live or work in the building being blessed.

After you have completed your blessing in the Health and Family area, move clockwise to the area related to Wealth and Prosperity. Here, you and all participants will follow the same basic steps as above, focusing on your hopes, wishes, and aspirations that are related to your wealth and prosperity.

Continue clockwise around to each of the Bagua areas. After Wealth and Prosperity, move to the area related to Fame and Reputation, then Love and Marriage, Children and Creativity, Helpful People and Travel, Career, and then Knowledge and Self-Cultivation. In each area, take all the time you need to light your candle, contemplate and focus on that particular area of your life, and then speak your good wishes aloud.

When you have gone through all eight Bagua areas, go to the center of the building where you will complete your Blessing. Light your last candle, silently review all the words that have been spoken, and feel the collected Ch'i surrounding you. It's important to get a sense of the blessed building as a living "being" whose purpose is to support and nurture you totally, and whose Ch'i you are in perfect harmony with now, and into the future. When you are ready, complete your Blessing with a final prayer, a verbal encapsulation of all that's been said, or a simple "Thank you" or "Amen."

Outdoor Bagua Blessings

Blessings can also be offered around the outside perimeter of a building. Classically, rice was used to bestow blessings upon the land around a structure, but since rice has been found to be harmful to birds, I use wild birdseed instead. Seeds symbolize all the potential and promise of new life. You can choose seeds of any kind, such as lawn grass, herbs, or wildflower seeds. As with the Indoor Blessing, you can do this alone, with others who live or work in the same building, and/or with friends who want to wish you well.

To prepare for an Outdoor Bagua Blessing, fill one small container with seeds for each participant. I use the red envelopes available at Chinese markets and gift stores, symbolizing the celebration of life. You can either use these, or decorate your own envelopes, bags, or pouches to symbolize your Blessing celebration. You will also need one candle for the center of the building, which can be placed there before the blessing begins, or carried throughout the blessing by one of the participants.

The Outdoor Blessing follows the same pattern as the Indoor Blessing. You begin by standing a comfortable distance away (four to eight feet or so) from the part of the building that is associated with Health and Family. Face the building, and take a few moments to contemplate what your prayers, wishes, hopes, and aspirations are for your health and family. When you are ready, voice them aloud. Other participants who live or work in the same building also take a turn to voice their thoughts and prayers. Any other participant is then invited to say a blessing related to Health and Family for the people living or working there.

After all blessings have been shared concerning Health and Family, everyone takes some of the seeds from their envelope and tosses them toward the building. This is a symbolic act of sealing in everyone's blessings and good wishes with the Ch'i of new life.

As with the Indoor Blessing, you proceed clockwise to the area of the building that is associated with Wealth and Prosperity. Again, take some time to contemplate, and then voice your hopes, goals, and good wishes for your wealth and prosperity. When you and all other participants are finished, toss more seeds toward the building's foundation, sealing in all the goodness of the moment, now and into the future. Then, continue clockwise to the areas associated with Fame and Reputation, then Love and Marriage, Creativity and Children, Helpful People and Travel, Career, and Knowledge and Self-Cultivation.

Ideally, your Outdoor Bagua Blessing is approached as a sacred time to literally and symbolically form a special relationship between yourself and the home or workplace you are blessing. It's a time to contemplate how well you are served by this dynamic living structure, and to seal in good fortune, happiness, and prosperity. Enjoy listening to yourself and others build the harmonious Ch'i with voiced blessings—Ch'i which is then sealed in forever through the symbol of new life, the seeds.

After you have blessed all eight external areas, move again to the center of the building. Your blessing is completed here by lighting your candle and silently reviewing all that has been said. As with the Indoor Blessing, bring your blessing to a close with a final prayer, an encapsulation of the blessings that have been shared, or a simple "Thank

You" or "Amen."

Bagua Blessings are often performed to celebrate any new beginning, such as a new house, new baby, new marriage, or new career. A time of contemplation and blessing aligns us with the structures that support us through life. A Bagua Blessing is also a wonderful way to gather strength during challenging or difficult times. The treasures of life, represented by the Bagua, are all connected, and in strengthening one, we strengthen them all.

We must reserve a back shop all our own, entirely free, in which to establish our real liberty and our principle retreat and solitude.

—*Michel Eyquem DeMontaigne*

10

HONORING PRIVACY AND BOUNDARIES

Just like vitamins and nutrients, privacy and personal boundaries are basic human needs. I don't know anyone who likes to find his or her desk rearranged by someone else, or who enjoys being stared at for any length of time. Our culture teaches us certain ways to relate to one another that may feel like violations to someone from another culture. For many of us in the West, it's uncomfortable to stand two inches away from someone and have a conversation, as many people from Middle Eastern countries do. We're used to having more space.

In the same way, our habit of making eye contact can be very disconcerting to people from certain Asian cultures. Within our own culture, our individual need for privacy and boundaries varies greatly. One person loves to be hugged and kissed, while another feels that the expression of casual affection infringes on his or her sense of personal boundaries.

We also have to consider that people living together—spouses, housemates, families—have different tastes in design. Add to that the fact that as people grow and change, they might want to modify their surroundings, in a way that someone else may not want. This issue can cause infringements on boundaries and lead to "turf wars."

Most of us can relate to the following stories that illustrate the importance of honoring people's privacy and personal boundaries.

ASKING PERMISSION

Nancy lived with her husband Sid in a 20th-century castle. No expense had been spared to create a 12,000-square-foot marble home of palatial proportions. Nancy had heard of Feng Shui at a party, and asked around for a local consultant. She was one of my first clients. When we made our appointment, it never occurred to me to ask her if Sid was interested in having his castle "Feng Shuied."

I arrived on a warm summer morning and was beeped through security gates that stood next to an artificial waterfall gushing down toward the street. I wondered why anyone would want to build a waterfall flowing away from the house. The Ch'i that plummeted down and away from the home was at least giving everyone who drove by a grand show. But much of the Ch'i that might have meandered benevolently throughout the property was being forcefully carried away.

Nancy answered my knock at the front entrance, opening 15-foot-high doors to let me in. Before me was a massive foyer that stretched into a wide hall leading to the rest of the house. Cool marble floors and walls enveloped me, and I wished I'd dressed more warmly.

I got the grand tour, moving from one spectacular room to another. Nancy's main complaint was that she and her husband didn't use many of the rooms. They lived in the kitchen, small den, and master bedroom.

"Look at this room, for instance," she said. "Even when we have company, we don't sit in this room."

We were standing at the door of a spacious living room. Everything there was in shades of white, with several dramatic pieces of metal sculpture on white pedestals. Two long white couches comprised the seating. Twenty-four large white pillows, packed in tight vertical rows, filled each couch.

"Forty-eight 'people' are already sitting in here, Nancy," I commented. "There's no room for anyone else to sit down."

"I never thought of it that way!" she exclaimed.

"And, this room is entirely made up of the Metal element," I commented. "It's time to bring in the colors and shapes of the other elements, especially Fire."

We proceeded to put 40 of the pillows away, leaving a generous 8 to accent the couches. Nancy brought out several large burgundy candles and placed them on the coffee table in crystal candleholders. The room began to come alive. Nancy caught the mood, and brought in colorful gifts and mementos that she loved for display on tables and wall shelves. Her choices introduced representations of all the elements, giving the room a new feeling of warmth and balance.

"Now I want to be in here!" she exclaimed.

Six hours later, we had made many changes and notes for more alterations throughout the house. We ended our session for the day, and planned to work with the Bagua during our next appointment.

When Sid came home to his castle that night, he immediately noticed that there'd been some changes made. Everywhere he looked, things were different.

"What the hell happened around here?" he asked, his eyes darting around the kitchen.

"Oh, I had a Feng Shui consultant come and work with the house today," Nancy answered.

"A what? What, are you crazy?! I didn't spent a fortune on a designer so that you could rearrange everything— you're gonna put every ?!#*?! thing back where it belongs, right now—I mean it!" Sid slammed out of the kitchen, and Nancy could hear him cursing as he went from room to room, finding our handiwork.

Now, she was upset. Why hadn't I mentioned that this could happen? So far, my visit had done nothing to enhance her marriage! As Sid continued to slam doors and verbally express his acute displeasure, Nancy called me and cancelled our second appointment. It was the last thing she needed! Forget the Bagua. It was going to take her days to calm her husband down. How dare I cause this problem in her life?!

Needless to say I learned my lesson. Practicing Feng Shui in the environment of someone who has not given permission, is very much like examining someone's body without his or her consent. Changing someone's environment is very personal, and, if done without permission, can feel like a violation. I now make sure that the okay has been given by everyone over the age of 12 who lives in the space I'll be working with. As a Feng Shui consultant, I make suggestions and comments on the rooms I'm invited to work in honoring the fact that it is up to the people who live or work there to carry out the changes—in their own time and in their own way.

▼▼▼

GREAT WHITE HUNTER

When Steve came home from Kenya and proudly unrolled the zebra skin he'd purchased there, his wife Sandy almost threw up. His trophy was one of the most disgusting things she'd ever seen! Steve absolutely loved it, though, and had planned on hanging it on the wall behind the living room sofa for everyone to enjoy. It was a big surprise to him that his wife didn't share his enthusiasm. They had a heated argument about where the skin was going to be placed in the house. Sandy wanted it out of the house completely, and Steve wanted it prominently displayed to remind him of his African journey. He felt so strongly about it that he went ahead and hung his prize over the sofa while Sandy was at work, figuring she would eventually learn to love it as much as he did. No such luck.

Sandy called me in tears, stating her case. She was sure that the Ch'i of a dead animal hanging in their living room must be terrible! I suggested that we get together so that I could talk with both her and Steve. When I pulled up to the house, I could see the zebra skin hanging over the sofa through the living room window. I guessed that everyone in the neighborhood knew that Steve had been to Africa by now.

Honoring boundaries can be very tricky territory. In this case, one person has had an experience that he is very excited about. He has a symbol of that adventure that he wants to display to the world, and his mate won't cooperate. In fact, his mate is quite offended by the symbol and doesn't want to have a thing to do with it. Now we have two people who feel violated, misunderstood, and angry. What do we do?

When at all possible, we divide and conquer. In other words, give each person their own territory. Draw a line around the perimeter of a space, however big or small, and anything inside that boundary is ruled exclusively by one person. They can do anything they please without environmental interference from the other!

In Sandy and Steve's case, they each claimed a room as their own territory. Steve already had a room he called his office in the house. But Sandy made her presence known there by changing or removing things that he wanted there whenever she pleased. Essentially, she didn't realize how important it was to honor Steve's room as his exclusive space. He'd been especially annoyed recently when she brought in a frilly bedroom lamp and replaced his office lamp with it, stating that she needed his good lamp in the living room.

Meanwhile, Sandy had never claimed a room in the house to be exclusively hers. She thought of the whole home as hers, including Steve's office. However, when she really examined her relationship with the house, she realized she didn't have anywhere that she could go and have some privacy to meditate, write a letter, or do creative projects. She supposedly "possessed" the whole house, yet none of it was exclusively hers. She decided to claim the guest room and lace it up with all "that feminine stuff" Steve disliked anywhere else in the house. Sandy's unhappiness dissipated rapidly as she entertained the notion of personalizing her own private space.

We took a look at Steve's office, which was in the Fame and Reputation area of the house. His desk was against a wall, with his chair facing away from the door. He had never thought of turning his desk around so that his chair would face the door, and he really took to the idea now. His beloved zebra could then have the entire wall behind him as its domain. Photographs he'd taken in Kenya would accent the other walls. Since one of the things that is correlated with the Bagua's Fame and Reputation area is the Fire element, which can be symbolized by animals, Steve's wild kingdom was well located there. And Sandy wasn't allowed to add to or subtract anything from his room. She promised she wouldn't as long as he didn't make fun of all her flowers and lace.

I left the Victorian lady and her great white hunter in peace, each of them relieved to have set some clear boundaries within their togetherness.

The Gift of Honoring Privacy and Boundaries

Whether you are married, a parent, a partner, or sharing a home or office with someone, define your own private space within that area. When this basic need isn't honored, turf wars, from subtle skirmishes to full-blown battles, can take place. Honor yourself by setting up a space you can call your own. And, honor those you live with by inviting them to do the same. The Ch'i in any household or workplace circulates in a much healthier, friendlier manner with this one simple adjustment.

Children as young as two years old will express their need for their own space. If a room is shared by siblings, help them both to set up a corner that is all theirs, with things that bring them joy, such as special toys, sports equipment, and stuffed animals. In a shared room, each child has his or her special spot that's honored as "off limits" to the other. The only way this concept works, though, is when it is taken seriously by the rest of the family. Little children learn early to understand that Mommy and Daddy need time alone if their own boundaries have also been honored.

Teenagers usually insist on their own turf. As in the story about Angie in the section on Knowledge and Self-Cultivation (page 145), teenagers can present big challenges to other family members as they catapult through puberty. Their private space is often chaotic and controversial. Typically, teenage chaos is active chaos—it changes as they change, and that happens often. In most cases, it's best to shut the door to their room for a few years and let the chaos run its course. However, as with Angie, intervention is sometimes necessary, and in most cases, can be offered as an observant suggestion rather than as an insistent demand. Again, the choice to honor each other's private place usually provides the space for harmony and balance to prevail.

A journey of a thousand
leagues starts from
where your feet stand.

—*Lao Tzu*

TRAVELING
FENG SHUI

In the midst of writing this book, my husband Brian and I decided to rent a cabin in a tiny mountain town to celebrate his birthday. We looked forward to retreating from our busy lives in San Diego to the quiet of the forest. We made reservations for our cabin based on a friend's referral, and soon we were on our way.

When we arrived, we discovered that our retreat was wonderful on the inside, but a mere ten feet from a well-traveled two-lane road. Needless to say, the peace and quiet we anticipated was shattered by the incessant loud whoosh of passing cars. It had never occurred to me to ask if our cabin would be practically in the middle of the street. All the other cabins were nicely tucked back into the woods, and all of them were occupied. We decided we would do our best to make the cabin's unfortunate location tolerable. We moved the bed from the front wall to the back, put candles and fresh flowers around the room, and played soft music, all of which helped to soften the dominance of the "raging river" road Ch'i. Still, we found it necessary to close the windows, shutting out both the traffic noise and the fresh pine-scented air we'd come to enjoy.

That experience inspired me to add this chapter on Traveling Feng Shui. Use the following information as a guide before you make reservations to stay anywhere you haven't been before.

First, decide exactly what kind of environment you prefer. Do you want a location that's private, quiet, and away from it all, or convenient and near a lot of activity (or a combination of both)? Be specific! Find out where driveways, roads, highways, and neighbors are, and if there are shopping centers, churches, and businesses nearby. In hotels, it's important to steer away from rooms located next to restaurants, bars, hospitality suites, ice and soda machines, elevator shafts, and so on— all potential problems.

Second, ask for a detailed description of the interior. What colors are predominant? You may not want to spend a weekend surrounded in vintage avocado green and rust brown. Along with the common questions such as what size is the bed and what electronic equipment (such as cable TV, VCR, and radio) is provided, ask if there are doors separating the bedroom and the bathroom, and if the windows open. Do they have a picture of the place that they can send you? Be as discerning about where you sleep as you are about the clothes you wear or the food you eat.

Whether you're planning a week's retreat in a rustic cabin, a month in a luxury condo, or a night in an economy lodge, a few extra minutes on the phone can spare you all kinds of problems on the other end. I've also noticed that friendly, helpful people, interested in answering all my questions, usually ensure a congenial, welcoming place with good Feng Shui.

Feng Shui Travel Kit

Sometimes we don't have the opportunity to book the perfect room. It may be a business trip where someone else has made all the arrangements, or there may be a language barrier. Whatever the reason, it's smart to travel with a Feng Shui Travel Kit. You can put a kit together yourself by choosing small, lightweight items that boost, balance, and circulate the Ch'i in any environment. For example, my Feng Shui Travel Kit consists of a small jewelry bag containing four round faceted crystals on strings, four small angels made of thick paper, four tealight candles in their own metal cups, and cleansing incense such as pine or sandalwood. These little Ch'i enhancers can transform a room from grim, to alive and agreeable. Also, in the kit are the necessary items for set-up: safety pins, paper clips, map tacks, string, and matches. I also pack a multicolored scarf that represents the colors of the five elements, and I'm ready to go.

Each room requires a different set-up. You can base your enhancements on the Bagua Map, using the door to the room as your entry point. I usually hang at least one crystal in the window and place candles and angels in my Health, Wealth, and Love areas. If the room feels "dead" or stagnant, I hang a crystal from the ceiling in the middle of the bedroom or the bathroom. I often set up one place of beauty on a table or bureau where I can rest my eyes and absorb the Ch'i. This spot can include my five-element cloth, incense, candles, angels, a bowl or glass of water, and fresh flowers or greenery when available. The idea is to travel with items that can quickly transform a questionable space into one that nourishes and takes care of you, even if only for one night. Choose items that are light and have them ready to go at a moment's notice.

Furniture on the Go

I am a notorious furniture re-arranger in my "homes away from home." If it's not nailed down, it's fair game! I find that it really wakes up and revitalizes the Ch'i to move at least one piece of furniture from the place it's been located for who knows how long. Think about how you would arrange the room if you were going to live there, and change it accordingly.

I also like to cover a prominently placed TV with a cloth, scarf, or towel and "put it to sleep," so to speak. Very few people are comfortable when they are being stared at, even if it's the single large black eye of a television.

Do whatever you need to feel as comfortable and at home as possible. You'll work better, rest better, and play better while preserving the integrity of your own vital Ch'i.

▼▼▼ ▼▼▼

Just trust yourself, then you
will know how to live.

—*Goethe*

12

SUMMARY – UNVEILING YOUR PARADISE

Feng Shui opens up a whole new world of seeing, listening to, and knowing about your environment. When you can "see" how the Ch'i moves through an area, "listen" to what it's saying, and know how to balance and improve its quality, your Feng Shui Eyes are open. You are free to create your own personal paradise—a place where you are surrounded by the environmental affirmations of your own choosing in the form of light, art, furniture, colors, patterns, nature objects, and architectural features. It's a place where vital Ch'i circulates harmoniously through each room, sustaining your home while inspiring, rejuvenating, comforting, and protecting you. It is a place that greets you with open arms and has the soft, nurturing qualities that melt away the stresses of the day. It is a place that "speaks" to you in a melodious and joyful language. *It is your place of peace.*

With Feng Shui, you can also arrange your workplace to be your springboard to success. You are free to create your personal power place—one where your furniture is chosen and arranged to bring out the best in you, putting you in the power seat, full of energy and motivation. It is a place where your desk is your game board, set up to win. It's a place where you put images and items that constantly focus you on the task at hand, stimulate your creativity, and support your goals and plans. Auspicious opportunities such as promotions, invitations, appointments, and advancements of all kinds are a part of your daily experience. It is a place where your vitality and charisma are constantly enhanced and supported by the lively circulation of Ch'i. *It is your place of power.*

Since no two homes, offices, people, days, or moments are alike, your challenge is not only to create ideal environments for yourself, but to keep them that way. Remember, the more dynamic your life is, the more dynamic your home and workplace will be. They are direct reflections of you. The Feng Shui adjustments and enhancements that you make today will need to be freshened, rearranged, and completely replaced from time to time. Your eyes need to remain fresh and alert to the dynamic dance around you.

Installing a water feature in the Wealth and Prosperity area with a surrounding flower garden may enhance your money flow and work beautifully for you. As time passes, however, it is important that you check your "fountain of fortune" regularly with your Feng Shui eyes, maintaining, adding to, and changing the area to accurately reflect who you are now. Whether it's changing the color or type of flowers, adding lighting, seating, or statuary, or changing the entire arrangement, be as creative as you like, and enjoy each composition you make. There is no end to the vibrant and inspiring combinations of things you can put together to enhance and refresh the Ch'i circulating around you.

No one solution lasts forever. What does last for all time is the dance between you and your environment—a dance that can continually bring great joy, opportunity, and prosperity into your life.

Enjoy!

▼▼▼ ▼▼▼

We make a vessel from a lump of clay;
It is the empty space within the vessel
   that makes it useful.
We make doors and windows for a
   room;
It is these empty spaces that make the
   room livable.
Thus, while the tangible has
   advantages,
It is intangible that makes it useful.

—Lao Tzu

APPENDIX

RECOMMENDED READING

All Sickness Is Home Sickness, Dianne M. Connelly. Columbia, MD: Traditional Acupuncture Institute, 1993

Care of the Soul, Thomas Moore. New York, NY: HarperCollins Publishers, 1992

Earth Design, Jami Lin. Miami Shores, FL: Earth Design, Inc., 1995

Feng Shui, Art and Harmony of Place, Johndennis Govert. Phoenix, AZ: Daikakuji Publications, 1993

The I Ching or Book of Changes, Richard Wilhelm. Translation by Cary F. Baynes. New York, NY: Princeton University Press, 1971

The Illustrated I Ching, R. L. Wing. New York, NY: Doubleday, 1982

Interior Design with Feng Shui, Sarah Rossbach. New York, NY: Arkana Books, 1987

Life! Reflections on Your Journey, Louise Hay. Carlsbad, CA: Hay House, Inc., 1995

Living Color, Sarah Rossbach and Lin Yun. New York, NY: Kodansha International, 1994

The Power of Place and Human Environments, anthology by James A. Swan. Wheaton, IL: Quest Books, 1991

The Seven Spiritual Laws of Success, Deepak Chopra. San Rafael, CA: New World Library, 1994

Tao Teh Ching, Lao Tzu. Translation by John C.H. Wu. Boston, MA: Shambhala Publications, 1961

You Can Have It All, Arnold Patent. Hillsboro, OR: Beyond Words Publishing, 1995

You Can Heal Your Life, Louise Hay. Carlsbad, CA: Hay House, 1984

You Can't Afford the Luxury of a Negative Thought, John Roger and Peter McWilliams. Los Angeles, CA: Prelude Press, 1988

ABOUT THE AUTHOR

Terah Kathryn Collins is a consultant, speaker, and teacher of Feng Shui residing in the San Diego area. She trained with Dr. Richard Tan, acupuncturist and Feng Shui expert in San Diego; Louis Audet, geomancer and Feng Shui specialist in Los Angeles; and Master Lin Yun, Feng Shui authority and founder of the Yun Lin Temple in Berkeley, California. Terah speaks regularly on Feng Shui to many special interest groups, and her classes on the subject are held in both San Diego and Washington, D.C.

With a background in communications and holistic health (as both a neurolinguistic programmer and a registered practitioner of polarity therapy), she effectively bridges the gap between mysterious Eastern practices and pragmatic Western thinking. Terah consults with both residential and commercial property owners, bringing the immense value of Feng Shui principles into their homes and businesses.

For information on career opportunities as a Feng Shui consultant, one-day Feng Shui workshops, and Feng Shui consultation services for residences and businesses, please call: **(619) 793-0945,** visit our website at: **http//www.wsfs.com,** or write: **Terah Kathryn Collins, c/o The Western School of Feng Shui, 437 South Highway 101, Suite 752, Solana Beach, CA 92075.**

THE WESTERN SCHOOL OF FENG SHUI™

THE WESTERN SCHOOL OF FENG SHUI offers practitioner training for men and women who are interested in becoming Feng Shui consultants or who want to add Feng Shui skills to their current career. Created by Terah Kathryn Collins, this unique program offers a comprehensive curriculum founded on the principles presented in *The Western Guide to Feng Shui.*

The program focuses on developing each student's intuitive, intellectual, and practical Feng Shui capabilities. Designed to open up whole new pathways of understanding, this holistic approach presents Feng Shui as both an intuitive art and a practical science. It also cultivates a dynamic blend of left- and right-brain skills. When combined with each individual's creative flair, these skills can bring tremendous benefits, satisfaction, and rewards to both practitioners and their residential and business clients.

"Feng Shui Marketing" is included as a vital component of the training. By providing proven and effective marketing tools, this program gives students the opportunity to turn their knowledge into real-world success.

Ultimately, anyone who feels committed to enriching his or her life or who wants to embark on a nurturing, supportive, and rewarding part- or full-time career path, will find this training to be a deeply meaningful, life-changing experience.

THE WESTERN SCHOOL OF FENG SHUI also offers Feng Shui consultation services for residences and businesses, and one-day Feng Shui workshops. For more information, please call:

**(619) 793-0945,
visit our website at: http//www.wsfs.com
or write: Terah Kathryn Collins
c/o The Western School of Feng Shui
437 South Highway 101, Suite 752
Solana Beach, CA 92075**

WESTERN SCHOOL OF FENG SHUI

Student Testimonials

"THE WESTERN SCHOOL OF FENG SHUI gave me excellent preparation for my Feng Shui career. This program is comprehensive, has a lot of integrity, and it's great fun. The trainers are also superb. Since graduating, I've been able to serve a growing list of clients with great confidence!"

— Becky Lott, Feng Shui consultant

"The training was fabulous! THE WESTERN SCHOOL OF FENG SHUI'S curriculum provides the insights and knowledge on a complicated subject and makes it easy to understand. This hands-on program has enabled me to provide a greater breadth of services to clients in my landscape design business. As a result, business is growing tremendously."

— Bridget Skinner, landscape architect, Feng Shui consultant

"This is the most comprehensive Feng Shui training for practitioners that I've found. Terah has put together an enjoyable and wonderful program that honors the mysticism of this ancient art, while it concentrates on in-depth practical applications. The Feng Shui Marketing aspect of the program is also invaluable. I feel confident, and my clients are seeing results!"

— Pamela K. Greer, Feng Shui consultant

"I learned many practical applications of Feng Shui principles that I now use with great success in my design practice. I would highly recommend this training to anyone who works with people and their environments."

— Cheryl Rice, ASID, interior designer

We hope you enjoyed this Hay House book.
If you would like to receive a free catalog featuring
additional Hay House books and products, or if you would like
information about the Hay Foundation, please contact:

Hay House, Inc.
P.O. Box 5100
Carlsbad, CA 92018-5100

(800) 654-5126
(800) 650-5115 (fax)

Please visit the Hay House Website at:
http://www.hayhouse.com